ANATOLE KONSTANTIN

AUTHOR OF

A Red Boyhood — Growing Up Under Stalin

Through the Eyes of an Immigrant

A BRIEF HISTORY OF COMMUNISM

THE RISE AND FALL OF THE SOVIET EMPIRE

D1569106

A Brief History of Communism

The Rise and Fall of the Soviet Empire

October 2017

Published by

Konstantin Memoirs, LLC

Norwalk, Connecticut

———◆———

ISBN 978-1-513623-69-6

Printed in the United States of America

A Brief History of Communism

The Rise and Fall of the Soviet Empire

To the memory of the countless millions of victims of Communism.

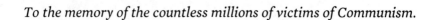

"If someone is coming to harm you, fight as hard as you can.
But if someone is coming to do you good, run as fast as you can."
A Russian Proverb

TABLE OF CONTENTS

PREFACE

This book is the story of the men who believed they knew how to create an ideal world and in its name did not hesitate to sacrifice millions of innocent lives. The book is written in conversational language by Anatole Konstantin, the author of *A Red Boyhood, Growing up under Stalin*, in which he describes his own experience of life in a Communist country.

On the 100th anniversary of the Russian Revolution in 1917, it is important to understand how a small band of Communists was able to take over a country of 150 million, and how, seventy-four years later, the huge Soviet Empire they had created, was exploded by three inebriated men.

The President of Russia, Vladimir Putin, has said that the demise of the Soviet Empire in 1991 was the greatest tragedy of the twentieth century. This book aims to show that the greatest tragedy of the century was the creation of this Empire in 1917.

Sign over the gate to the worst Siberian Gulag:

WITH AN IRON FIST

WE WILL LEAD HUMANITY

TO HAPPINESS

KEY FIGURES:

Karl Marx – The principal creator of the Communist idea.

Vladimir Lenin – The first Communist Dictator and a mass murderer.

Joseph Stalin – The second Communist Dictator and a mass murderer.

Leon Trotsky – The Organizer of the Red Army and a mass murderer.

Feliks Dzerzhinsky – The Organizer of the secret police and a mass murderer.

Lavrenti Beria – Head of the KGB and a mass murderer, executed by Khrushchev.

Nikita Khrushchev – A mass murderer; loved Lenin, hated Stalin.

Mikhail Gorbachev – The reformer and last president of the Soviet Union.

IN THEIR OWN WORDS

KARL MARX

"The last capitalist we hang will be the one who sold us the rope."

VLADIMIR LENIN

"Hang, I mean hang publicly so that people see it, at least a hundred kulaks. . . so that for miles around people see it all, understand, tremble, and tell themselves that we will continue to do so. . ."

IN THEIR OWN WORDS

JOSEPH STALIN

"The death of one person is a tragedy, the death of a million is a statistic."

"Shoot at least twenty or thirty of the saboteurs who managed to infiltrate these organizations."

LEON TROTSKY

"The Red Terror is a weapon used against a class that, despite being doomed to destruction, does not wish to perish."

IN THEIR OWN WORDS

FELIX DZERZHINSKY

"For many people there is nothing so frightening as my name."

"The most effective is taking of hostages among the bourgeoisie. . . and incarceration. . . in a concentration camp."

LAVRENTY BERIA

"Give me any man for three days, and he will admit he is the Prince of Wales."

IN THEIR OWN WORDS

NIKITA KHRUSHCHEV

When asked what he regretted about his life:

"Most of all the blood. My arms are up to the elbows in blood."

MIKHAIL GORBACHEV

"Our people and the country's leaders understood that we could no longer continue as we had. . ."

"Russia will prosper. . . only if it follows a democratic path."

MAP OF THE SOVIET UNION

Chapter 1
How It All Began

In 1818, a son was born into a lawyer's family in the German city of Trier. His name was Karl Heinrich Marx. He was kicked out of university for drunkenness and dueling with swords, which at that time was the ultimate macho deed of students, and had to finish his studies at another school. He was arrogant, did not tolerate contradiction, and wrote that "while the philosophers have only interpreted the world, the point is to CHANGE IT." And he believed he knew how to do it.

To Karl Marx, mankind was divided into two classes: the capitalist class that owned businesses and land and lived in luxury, and the proletarian class, the workers and peasants who produced everything but lived in misery. Therefore, to make the world just, the workers should revolt and establish a dictatorship of the proletariat that would make everything owned jointly by everyone.

Karl Marx expected that capitalists and landowners would not give up their possessions voluntarily, and believed they should be eliminated as a class, like it was done during the French Revolution some fifty years before, when people were guillotined just for belonging to the class of nobility. He also believed the greedy capitalists would cooperate in their own destruction, and is said to have written: "The last capitalist we hang, shall be the one who sold us the rope."

He became an editor of a radical magazine and when he feared he might be arrested, escaped to France. There he met another German, Friedrich Engels, who, in spite of his wealthy family owning textile factories in England, was also a revolutionary, and together they founded the Communist League.

What kind of a person was this man who wanted to change the world? While his earnings were inadequate to support a wife and seven children, he said he did not want to let the capitalist society make a "money-making machine" out of him. However, he did not hesitate to take "capitalist" money from his friend Engels, who to discourage theft in the mail tore it in half and mailed the halves separately. Engels was such a good friend, that when the great moralizer Marx got his maid pregnant, to save him embarrassment the bachelor Engels claimed that the child was his.

In 1848, which, due to a wave of revolts in several European countries was very turbulent, the Communist League published *The Communist Manifesto*. It called on the workers of the world to revolt, unite, and establish a worldwide "dictatorship of the proletariat." They wrote: "Let the ruling classes tremble at a Communist revolution.... When our turns comes, we shall make no excuses for the terror."

There must have been many people wishing to take over someone else's property, because Marxist parties sprung up in many countries waiting for an opportune moment to do so. In Russia, that moment came in 1917, towards the end of World War I.

HOW DID THE COMMUNISTS DO IT?

The leader of the Russian Communists was not someone from the working class, but a Marxist lawyer named Vladimir Lenin for whom promises were just tools for reaching his objectives.

To the peasants, the Communists promised to confiscate the land of large landowners and distribute it to them. They did not mention their intention to take it away later and to force the peasants into collective farms.

To the factory workers, they promised to nationalize the factories, railroads, mines, and other businesses, and have them managed by workers committees. Since the factories would belong to the government that represented all the people, the workers would then be working for themselves.

To the soldiers and sailors, who were being slaughtered by the millions, they promised an immediate end of the war. They would make peace with Germany and Austria, and the soldiers and sailors could go home to their families. They did not tell them that they would then be drafted again to fight on the side of the Communists in the Civil War.

To the young people, they promised an unlimited future. Once the private property and the capitalist class were eliminated, an ideal classless Communist society would come to pass, in which all would be equal and would receive everything they needed from the government. In return, they would contribute to this society according to their ability.

WHO WAS LENIN?

His real name was Vladimir Ilych Ulyanov and he was born in 1870 into a well-to-do family. His father was a superintendent of schools, and his mother owned a small estate. According to an article in *The New York Times* of May 8, 2012: "As a baby, Lenin had a head so large that he often fell over. He used to bang his head on the floor, making his mother worry that he might be mentally disabled."

When Vladimir was seventeen, his older brother Alexander was involved in a failed plot to assassinate the Tsar. The conspirators were arrested and sentenced to death, but the lives of those who pleaded for mercy were spared. Alexander however refused to plead and was hanged.

At the University, Vladimir became involved in revolutionary activity and was expelled, and, like Karl Marx, received his law degree from another school. In 1895 he went to Switzerland, where he met leaders of the Russian Marxist Social Democratic Party in exile. He joined the party and was caught when he tried to smuggle its revolutionary literature back to Russia. In prison, the political prisoners could use a library, and his mother was allowed to bring him books, food, and clothing. She also smuggled out his revolutionary writings.

After a year in prison, Lenin was exiled for three years to a remote village in Siberia, to which he proceeded on his own by train, on horseback, and by a river boat, which took him more than two months. There he went hunting, visited friends who had been exiled to nearby villages, studied languages, and wrote a book. In 1898, his fiancé, Nadezhda Krupskaya, also a revolutionary exiled for three years, arrived, and they were married. His exile ended in 1900, and he went to Geneva, Switzerland, where he joined the Social Democrat leadership. These details of how the Tsarist government treated its political dissidents are important for comparison with how Lenin later would treat his opponents.

In 1903, Lenin, who by then had assumed his revolutionary name, went with some sixty Russian delegates to the Social Democratic Congress in London. The main issue at the Congress was whether the party should organize itself as a democracy in which anyone could participate in decision-making, or if all decision-making should be given to a central committee? Lenin, who, like Marx was arrogant and did not tolerate being contradicted, insisted on a central committee. He contrived to lock his opponents out of various meetings, and his proposal won by two votes.

In Russian, the word "majority" is *bolshinstvo,* and because of these two votes, Lenin's faction began calling itself the Bolsheviks, a word that for seventy years terrorized millions of people.

The losing group, called the Mensheviks, from the Russian word for "minority", also wanted to eliminate private property, but to do it not by violence but by democratic means. There were several other parties demanding change in Russia: the non-Marxist Social Revolutionaries whose goal was distribution of land to the peasants; the Constitutional Democrats, who wanted to limit the absolute power of the Tsar by a constitution; the Anarchists, who did not want any government at all; and several smaller groups.

RUSSIA IN 1917

Between 1880 and 1914 when World War I began, the Russian economy was growing at the rate of 6 to 7 percent, which was the highest in Europe. Foreign investments were coming into mining, steel, textiles, sewing machines, farm equipment, locomotives, and railroads, which by 1912 were second only to those in the United States.

Russian agriculture supplied grain to Europe, and in St. Petersburg, Igor Sikorsky had built the world's first four-engine airplane.

In 1894, Tsar Nicolas II had succeeded his father Alexander III, and a feast celebrating his coronation was prepared for 100,000 people, with free food, beer, and souvenirs. When the gates to the feast were opened the crowd rushed in and in the stampede close to 1,400 were trampled to death. Tsar Nicolas was upset, but this did not prevent him from attending the coronation ball that evening, which did not go over well with the public.

Then, in the 1905 war with Japan, Russia suffered a humiliating defeat that demonstrated the incompetence of the regime. Russia was much larger than Japan and had a much larger army. It also had a larger fleet, but it was decimated in a battle in the Straits of Tsushima. Because the Straits were narrow, the Russian ships had to proceed through it single-file, and the Japanese fleet that waited for them at the exit, blasted the Russian ships as they appeared one at a time and sank 20 of them, with the loss of 12,000 men. The Japanese lost three torpedo boats and 120 men. For helping to negotiate the peace agreement between Russia and Japan, the American President Theodore Roosevelt received the Nobel Peace Prize.

The defeat in this war added to the unrest among industrial workers, and on Sunday, January 22, 1905, some 200,000 men, women, and children, were led by a priest to present to the Tsar a petition asking for higher pay and an eight-hour work day. They carried icons and pictures of the Tsar and sang the national hymn "God Save the Tsar." But when army officers ordered the procession to halt, it could not stop under pressure from those behind, and the soldiers opened fire, killing about 1,000 and injuring many more.

As a result of this "Bloody Sunday," there were industrial strikes organized by worker's councils, known as the "soviets," and also peasants' revolts in which land-owners were murdered and their estates burned. There were also mutinies in the army and the navy, and Lenin secretly returned to Russia from Switzerland and attempted to organize an armed uprising. His activities were financed by wealthy opponents of the Tsar, and by bank robberies like those in Georgia, committed by a revolutionary named Koba, who would later become known as Joseph Stalin. When the police began closing in on Lenin, he again escaped abroad.

As the disorders continued, there was a strong popular reaction blaming them on minorities, which in some areas resulted in pogroms on Jews, many of whom then fled the country for the United States and South America. To quell the disorders, the Tsar declared martial law, but it would still take two years before order was restored completely.

Hoping to avoid repetition of the revolts, the Tsar announced the formation of an elected representative assembly called the State Duma, but it fell short of establishing a constitutional monarchy like that in England. Nevertheless, the Prime Minister of the Duma, Pyotr Stolypin, introduced significant reforms including universal education, recognition of trade unions, health and accident insurance for workers, and the promotion of homesteading in Siberia. But the radicals, fearing that these reforms would improve living conditions and forestall the revolution, assassinated Stolypin just as they had killed Tsar Alexander II, who in 1861 had abolished serfdom.

Politically, there were no restrictions on foreign books other than the revolutionary pamphlets published abroad by exiled radicals, and there were numerous active unofficial groups of students and intellectuals, including

Marxist Socialists. In St. Petersburg alone, students could attend one of the more than twenty Marxist discussion groups, and revolutionary agitation and propaganda among industrial workers, peasants, students, and in the armed forces, continued at a high rate.

The difference between agitation and propaganda was explained by Lenin as follows:

> A propagandist . . . must give many ideas concentrated all together, so many that all of them will not be understood by the average person . . . . The agitator, on the other hand, will pick out one or more of less familiar and concrete aspects of the entire problem. His efforts will be concentrated on this fact to implant to the masses a single idea . . . . He will try to evoke among the masses discontent and revolt against this great injustice and will leave the explanation for this contradiction to the propagandist.

Whom, as he had said before, no one understood.

THE DEMOCRATIC REVOLUTION OF FEBRUARY 1917

On June 28, 1914, the Austrian Archduke Franz Ferdinand was assassinated by a Serbian nationalist in Sarajevo, and Austria issued to Serbia an ultimatum demanding the right to station its troops on Serbian territory. As Russia was a protector of Slavic Serbia, Nicholas II ordered the mobilization of its army against Austria. Then, Austria's ally Germany issued an ultimatum to Russia demanding that it demobilize its army within twelve hours, and on August 1, 1914, declared war on Russia and its allies France and England.

The Russian Army had 4.5 million men and initially the war was popular. However, a year later, after several defeats and severe shortages of food and fuel, there was general discontent both in the Army and in the country, and as the military situation continued to deteriorate the Tsar took over command and went to the front. This was a big mistake, because he then became personally responsible for any defeats, and could not blame them on incompetent generals.

The Tsar left his wife Alexandra in charge of the government, but the fact that she had been a German princess raised questions about her loyalty to Russia. Also, she was under the influence of a self-anointed "holy man" with burning and penetrating eyes, named Grigori Rasputin, who — presumably by his hypnotic personality — was able to relieve the bleeding of her hemophiliac son.

Rasputin was a huge crude peasant who was perpetually drunk, and a great womanizer. His line with the ladies was that in order to be saved one had to repent, but in order to repent one had first to commit a sin, and he was ready to help them to do that. According to reports by the police that followed him, this line was successful with the ladies of the court as well as with their maids. But Alexandra had complete faith in Rasputin's holiness, and on his advice even replaced government ministers with those recommended by the corrupt Rasputin.

There were rumors that both Rasputin and Alexandra were betraying Russia, and he was hated by people high and low. On December 31, 1916, several aristocrats invited him for New Year's Eve dinner and gave him wine poisoned with strychnine. When this proved ineffective, they shot him four times, but he still managed to get out of the house and fall into a canal where he disappeared under the ice and his body was not found until the next day.

As the war dragged on, military defeats, desertions by soldiers, food riots and strikes continued to grow, and when in February of 1917 the army in St. Petersburg revolted and refused to suppress the disorders, Nicholas II abdicated the throne in favor of his brother, Duke Michael. However, the duke refused to accept the title of emperor unless a Constitutional Assembly voted to retain the monarchy.

In the absence of a head of state, the Duma took over the ministries and formed a Provisional Government to prepare elections to the Constitutional Assembly. The Provisional Government continued the war against Germany but, in spite of the help from England, France, and the United States, the war was not going well.

The Provisional Government was democratic, in which several political parties were trying to outmaneuver one another. With continuous strikes organized by the Communists, peasant revolts, desertions from the army, and the growing shortages of food and fuel, the government leadership changed every couple of months, and was unable to control the situation.

THE BOLSHEVIK COUP

When the news that the Tsar had abdicated reached Lenin in Zurich, he contacted the German Ambassador and promised that if Germany helped him return to Russia, he would see to it that Russia got out of the war, which would allow Germany to move all its forces to the Western Front. On March 31st, the German ambassador sent a coded telegram to Berlin saying: "Urgent! The journey of the Russian émigrés through Germany should take place very quickly since the Entente (England, France, and Italy) has already started countermeasures in Switzerland. Speed up the negotiations as much as possible."

To maintain secrecy, Lenin and his group traveled through Germany in a sealed railroad car, and on April 16 reached St. Petersburg, which would soon be renamed Petrograd because "burg" is a German word. The Communists did not waste any time urging overthrow of the Provisional Government and an immediate peace with Germany. They demanded that all power be handed over to the "Soviets" (committees) of Workers, Soldiers, and Peasants. Since the Bolsheviks were the best-organized party, they were able to disrupt the economy by continuous strikes, demonstrations, and riots, and gained control of most of the Soviets.

Lenin unsuccessfully attempted to overthrow the Provisional Government in April, June, and July, but after his dealings with the Germans became known, he was accused of being a German agent and went into hiding in Finland. From there he planned and directed the Bolshevik's actions, and wrote:

> In a time of revolution, it is not enough to ascertain the 'will of majority'. . . we see countless instances of how the better organized, more conscious, better-armed minority imposed its will on the majority and conquered it.

Then, on the night of November 6, 1917, as the Provisional Government was meeting at the Tsar's Winter Palace guarded only by a Women's Battalion because the regular army units were at the front, bands of Bolshevik Red Guards together with army deserters and mutinous sailors, stormed the palace and dispersed the government.

By the morning of November 7, the Bolsheviks had seized the railway stations, the state bank, the power station, the telephone exchange, and the bridges across the river. The Bolsheviks called it the October Revolution, because, by the Julian calendar still used in Russia at that time, it was October 25th. In reality, it was not a revolution but a coup – a takeover by a small group by force, without the participation of the population. The actual revolution had happened in February when the Tsar had abdicated, and the democratic Provisional Government had taken over the country. The American correspondent John Reed, who was there, described these events in his book *Ten Days That Shook the World.*

Within days of the Bolshevik coup, Lenin set up a political police — the Cheka, a Russian abbreviation for "extraordinary commission" — that began arresting members of the Provisional Government and seizing the printing presses of opposing political parties so that they could not communicate with the population.

But, believing that they would gain the majority that would give the coup legitimacy, the Bolsheviks did not cancel the election to the Constitutional Assembly. The election was held on November 25, and when out of 41.7 million votes the Bolsheviks received only 9.8 million, or only about 24 percent, they decided to sabotage the Assembly, and their new slogan became: "DOWN WITH THE CONSTITUTIONAL ASSEMBLY – ALL POWER TO THE SOVIETS!"

The big winners of the election with 58 percent of the vote, were the Social Revolutionaries, the radical peasant party, but their followers were not armed, and they could not enforce their policies. On December 26, Lenin wrote in the Bolshevik newspaper *Pravda* that the interests of the revolution "stand over the formal rights of the Constitutional Assembly . . . The Russian Republic is vested with the Soviets . . . Every attempt to usurp the government authority . . . will be suppressed."

When on January 18, 1918, as a large demonstration carrying placards demanding "All power to the Constitutional Assembly" was approaching the imperial palace where the assembly was to take place, it was fired upon by the Red Guards. Inside the palace, the corridors and galleries were packed with heavily armed Red Guards and Bolshevik sailors. Lenin himself brought a pistol, but someone stole it from him.

Every speech by the delegates was interrupted by the Bolsheviks singing their anthem, the "Internationale", and by whistles, catcalls, and shouts. Lenin pretended to have fallen asleep. After six or seven hours of this, the Bolshevik motion that the Assembly recognize the Congress of Soviets (that was controlled by them) as the government of Russia, was defeated 237 to 136. Then the Red Guards turned off the lights.

On the next day, January 19, 1918, the Executive Committee of the Bolshevik Congress of Soviets passed a resolution dissolving the Constitutional Assembly, and armed guards were posted at its doors. Lenin later wrote, "The dissolution of the Constitutional Assembly by the Soviet Government means a complete and frank liquidation of the idea of democracy by the idea of dictatorship."

This is how a well-organized armed band of Bolsheviks, guided by an energetic, decisive and unscrupulous leader, gained control of a city of two million.

CHAPTER 2
THE CHAOS

With the Bolsheviks now in control of Petrograd, they had to figure out how to gain control over the rest of the nation of around 150 million people, that extended over eleven time zones from the Pacific Ocean to the Baltic Sea.

The overall power in the Soviet government was held by the Central Executive Committee of the Communist Party under Lenin, which set up the Soviet (Council) of People's Commissars, all of whom were Communists. The military power rested in the Petrograd Revolutionary Military Committee, which in the first fifty-three days issued more than 6,000 orders signed by more than twenty people claiming to be its chairman and issuing uncoordinated and often contradictory orders.

On November 8, 1917, the day after the Bolsheviks took power, all non-Communist newspapers were closed, and all radio and telegraph stations were taken over by the Bolshevik Red Guards. On November 13, the Military Committee proclaimed that "High-ranking functionaries in state administration, banks, the Treasury, the railways and post and telegraph offices are all sabotaging the measures of the Bolshevik Government. Henceforth such individuals are to be described as 'enemies of the people.'" Few days after that it announced that "All individuals suspected of sabotage, speculation, and opportunism are now liable to be arrested immediately."

According to the Communists, speculators were the businessmen who sold something for more than they had paid for it, which meant all shopkeepers, including those who sold food. And, since Lenin had declared, ". . . as long as we fail to treat speculators thc way they deserve — with a bullet in the head — we will not get anywhere at all", who was going to supply the food?

WHO WAS GOING TO SUPPLY FOOD?

On November 17, ten days after taking power, Lenin established a Food Commission, whose job it was "to requisition the surpluses of the rich, and all their goods as well." Special detachments of Red Guards were dispatched to the provinces "to procure food needed in Petrograd and at the front," giving them permission, in effect, to pillage in the name of the revolution.

Three weeks after taking power, on November 28, Lenin ordered the arrest of all leaders of the Constitutional Democratic Party. They were to be brought before a People's Revolutionary Court, which, according to the People's Commissar of Justice, was not "a court in the normal 'bourgeois' sense, but a court of dictatorship of the proletariat." Many of those arrested were jailed in the same prisons in which they sat under the Tsar, and initially expected the same treatment they had received from the Tsar's police: newspapers, books, writing paper, visits and packages from relatives. But such illusions did not last long — Lenin was not going to make the same mistake in treating his opponents that the Tsar's government had made in treating him. Those demanding all this were put into a solitary confinement cell or shot.

As the Communist Party explained how to conduct investigations:

> We are not waging war against individuals, we are exterminating bourgeoisie as a class. During the investigation, do not look for evidence that the accused acted in word or deed against Soviet power. The first questions that you ought to put are: To what class does he belong? What is his origin? What is his education or profession? And it is these questions that ought to determine the fate of the accused.

This is the exact procedure that many years later was followed by the Cambodian Communist Dictator Pol Pot when he killed about two million people — a quarter of the Cambodian population.

After the Cheka cruelly suppressed a strike by state employees, the People's Commissar of Justice said to Lenin that it would be more honest to call him the People's Commissar for Social Extermination. To which Lenin replied that this is exactly how he sees it, but it would not do to call him that.

Within the first two months of the Bolshevik takeover, some 15,000 were executed by the Cheka, while during the ninety-two years before the Tsar abdicated, the Tsarist courts had pronounced only 6,321 death sentences for political offenses. To head the Cheka killing machine, Lenin appointed Felix Dzerzhinsky, whom he had met in exile.

WHO WAS DZERZHINSKY?

Felix Dzerzhinsky was born a Polish nobleman and, like Lenin, the son of a teacher. He had six siblings and one day, when he and his brother were playing with a rifle, they accidentally killed their fourteen-year-old sister. He dropped out of school, became a Marxist agitator, and wrote poetry. In 1898, at the age of twety one, he was arrested and sent into exile in a northern village where, also like for Lenin, his girlfriend was allowed to follow him. He was permitted to hunt, and for recreation he trained a pet bear. The following year he escaped but was rearrested, and by 1912 had escaped three more times. After his next arrest, he was put in chains and was not released until after the 1917 Revolution. But even in prison, he received newspapers and money from his siblings. Also like Lenin, he was not going to make with his prisoners the same mistake that the Tsar's government had made with him.

The Cheka began with 100 people. Perhaps because Dzerzhinsky did not think that ethnic Russians would be hard enough on their fellow Russians, his recruits were mostly from Poland and the Baltic states. Dzerzhinsky described them as having "burning hearts and clear heads." He himself had a burning heart and penetrating eyes, and in 1919 wrote to one of his sisters: "For many people, there is nothing so frightening as my name."

Dzerzhinsky's men were either fanatics or sadists or both. His female interrogators were especially feared because they mutilated men's genitals. In his book *Stalin and his Hangmen,* Donald Rayfield wrote about one of them in Odessa, who in two and a half months mutilated 700 prisoners before having them shot.

The dreaded trademark uniforms of the Cheka were leather coats that had been shipped for the Tsar's air force pilots, and which Dzerzhinski had appropriated. As the Cheka spread into every province, it became the major execution instrument of the government, hunting down members of the opposition parties and suppressing strikes by workers and riots by peasants who were being robbed not only of the grain needed for their food but also that needed for seeds.

The same Bolsheviks, who only months before had urged workers to strike for better conditions, were now executing the strikers for making the same demands, accusing them of sabotaging the revolution. In March 1919, when the workers from the Putilov factory who had stormed the Winter Palace and helped disperse the Provisional Government went out on strike, the Cheka arrested around 900 strikers and executed more than 200 without a trial.

LENIN AND GERMANY

As Lenin had promised the Germans, ceasefire negotiations with them began on December 28, 1917, in the city of Brest-Litovsk. But, when the Commissar of Foreign Affairs, Leon Trotsky, did not accept their conditions, the German army advanced, and Lenin moved the capital from Petrograd to Moscow, where his proletarian government settled in the Tsar's Kremlin. The treaty signed on March 3, 1918, handed Ukraine, Belarus, and the Baltic states over to Germany.

The Allied countries, who had been supplying the Russian armies with large quantities of armaments and ammunition through the sea ports of Archangel, Murmansk, and Vladivostok, did not want these supplies to fall into Bolshevik hands and landed in these ports to retrieve the stockpiled materials. The Bolshevik propagandists immediately claimed that the United States, Britain, and France were invading Russia, and called for resistance to the interventionists.

Without the food-producing Ukraine, Belarus and the Baltic States — Estonia, Lituania, and Latvia — bread rations were decreased to four ounces a day. As discontent grew among Lenin's previous supporters, Lenin, fearing an uprising, decreed that:

> Every factory, every company must set up its own requisitioning detachments. Everyone must be mobilized in the search for bread, not simply volunteers but absolutely everyone; anyone who fails to cooperate will have his ration card confiscated immediately.

What did it mean "to set up its own requisitioning detachments?" It meant that every factory was ordered to send squads of thugs to the countryside to rob peasants of whatever food they had, which included grain they needed for planting the following spring. The better-off peasants who had hired help were called "kulaks," and, since they would have more grain than the poor peasants, they were the first victims of the marauding requisitioners.

Leon Trotsky, who in addition to being already the Commissar for Foreign Affairs and the War Commissar, was now also appointed the head of the Extraordinary Commission for Food and Transport. He announced that:

> In less than a month (the) terror is going to take extremely violent forms, just as it did in the great French Revolution. Not only prison awaits our enemies, but the guillotine, that remarkable invention of the French Revolution which has the capacity to make a man a whole head shorter.

WHO WAS TROTSKY?

Leon Trotsky was born in 1879 on a prosperous farm in Ukraine, and in 1897 attended Odessa University where he studied mathematics. There he became involved in organizing the Southern Ukrainian Worker's Union, for which he was arrested in 1898 and sentenced to four years in Siberia, from where he escaped in 1902. He went abroad, where he met Lenin, and wrote articles for a Marxist newsletter. In 1905, he returned to Russia to participate in the revolution and was rearrested. This time he was sentenced to exile in Siberia for life, but escaped on the way there and settled in France, where he wrote articles against the war, for which in 1914 was deported to Spain, from where he made his way to New York.

After the February 1917 revolution, Trotsky embarked for Russia but was detained by the British authorities in Canada and interned in a prisoner-of-war camp. He was freed at the request of the Russian Provisional Government, which in October, as a leader of the Bolshevik Military Revolutionary Committee, he helped to destroy. Trotsky was a Marxist theorist, and advocated the idea of a Permanent Revolution, which he described as the Bolshevik revolution that "begins on a national arena, unfolds on the international arena and is completed on the world arena." His objective was a world revolution of which Russia was only the starting point. He was a fiery orator, which made him a persuasive agitator. His vision of the new Bolshevik man's future was that: "Man will make it his purpose . . . to raise himself to a new plane, to create a higher social biologic type, if you please, a superman."

THE RED TERROR

In the summer of 1918, there were 140 peasant revolts against the forcible confiscation of food, as they were allowed to keep only about one-tenth of what was needed to survive. But Lenin called these revolts "kulak" rebellions and ordered that "In all grain-producing areas, twenty-five designated hostages drawn from the best-off of the local inhabitants will answer with their lives for any failure in the requisitioning plan."

In a telegram of August 9, 1918, to regional Soviets, Lenin added, "You (must) establish a dictatorial troika and introduce mass terror, shooting and deporting the hundreds of prostitutes who are causing all the soldiers to drink, all ex-officers, etc. . . . . You must act resolutely with massive reprisals. Immediate execution for anyone caught in possession of firearms."

It is difficult to imagine that anyone believed the Russian soldiers needed someone to encourage them to drink. The state of Lenin's bloodthirsty mind is shown by his telegram on the next day:

> You must make an example of these people (kulaks). (1) Hang (I mean hang publicly so that people see it) at least hundred kulaks, rich bastards, and known blood-suckers. (2) Publish their names. (3) Seize all their grain. (4) Single out the hostages per my instructions in yesterday's telegram. Do all this, so that for miles around people see it all, understand it, tremble, and tell themselves that we are killing the bloodthirsty kulaks and that we will continue to do so. Reply, saying that you have received and carried out these

instructions. Yours, Lenin. P.S. Find tougher people.

Who were the "tougher" people who enjoyed hanging someone? They were sadistic criminals who were now being put in power by Lenin — the man Soviet propaganda later depicted as the greatest humanitarian in the history of mankind.

On July 17, 1918, on Lenin's orders, the Tsar and his family were murdered. On August 30, a Social Revolutionary woman named Fanya Kaplan, shot and wounded Lenin. She was executed three days later, together with 500 hostages.

On September 5, the Bolshevik government issued a decree entitled "On Red Terror" which stated that, 'in order to protect the Soviet Republic from its class enemies, they must all be locked up in concentration camps.' Bolshevik leader Grigory Zinoviev, who himself was later executed by Stalin, explained:

> To dispose of our enemies, we will have to create our own socialist terror. For this, we will have to train 90 million of the 100 million Russians and have them all on our side. We have nothing to say to the other 10 million; we will have to get rid of them.

Since the peasants now had no incentive to produce food that would be taken away from them, the food situation continued to worsen. At the end of 1919, industrial workers were receiving special rations of half a pound of bread a day. Their salaries were between 7,000 and 12,000 rubles a month, while on the black market a pound of butter cost 5,000 rubles, a pound of meat 3,000 and a pint of milk 500.

In May 1919, the newspaper *Izvestia* announced that:

> The property owning classes will be required
> to fill in a questionnaire detailing foodstuffs,
> shoes, clothes, jewels, bicycles, bedding,
> sheets, silverware, crockery, and other articles
> indispensable to the working population . . . .
> It is the duty of all to assist the expropriation
> commissions in this sacred task. Anyone failing
> to assist the expropriation commissions will be
> arrested immediately. Anyone resisting will be
> executed without further delay.

The next phase of expropriations was the confiscation
of apartments and homes of "bourgeoisie," leaving the
owner's family only one room, and bringing in a family to
each room of an apartment or a house.

While taking hostages to guarantee food deliveries
became a standard practice in 1918, in 1919 Lenin signed
a decree ordering that hostages be taken also for non-
political problems such as clearing snow from railroad
tracks: "And if the lines aren't swept properly, the hostages
are to be shot."

CHAPTER 3
HOW COMMUNISTS WON THE CIVIL WAR

The resistance to the Communists in various regions of the country turned into a civil war. Fighting the Bolshevik Red Army were the White Army of the Tsar, the Green Army of the Ukrainian Nationalists, the Black Army of the Ukrainian Anarchists, the White Cossack Army, and many other armed groups.

The national minorities, to whom the Bolsheviks initially promised independence, organized their own nationalist armies. Also, the political parties that were being exterminated, the starving workers who were forbidden to strike, the peasants who rebelled against food requisitions, the bands of anarchists and deserters, and even Czech prisoners of war — all took up arms against the Bolsheviks. However, in addition to fighting the Communists, they frequently also fought one another. As control of cities, towns, and villages, changed hands again and again (Kiev changed hands fourteen times), the various groups killed their real or imaginary enemies, and many took the opportunity to stage pogroms on Jews.

With so many fighting against the Bolsheviks, how did they manage to win the Civil War? The main reason was that their enemies were not united and the Bolsheviks were able to send an overwhelming force against one group at a time. But how did the Bolsheviks get the overwhelming force?

It was Leon Trotsky who organized the Red Army and led Bolsheviks to victory. By ending the war with Germany, Trotsky had won over some of the Tsarist soldiers to the Bolshevik's cause. But, when during the Civil War he did not have enough fighters, he began conscripting peasants into the Red Army and to make them fight threatened to have their families shot if the soldiers had deserted. He did the same thing with Tsarist officers, each of whom was then watched by a Bolshevik commissar. This is how by sheer terror he made anti-Communists fight for the Communists.

In his autobiography, Trotsky wrote:

> An army cannot be built without reprisals. Masses of men cannot be led to death unless the army command has the death penalty in its arsenal. So long as those malicious tailless apes that are so proud of their technical achievements — the animal that we call men — will build armies and wage wars, the command will always be obliged to place the soldiers between the possible death in the front and inevitable one in the rear. . . . I issued an order (that) was distributed throughout the army: 'I give warning that if any unit retreats without orders, the first to be shot will be the commissar of the unit, and the next the commander . . . . Cowards, dastards and traitors will not escape the bullet.'

These were not empty threats. Trotsky set up special punitive brigades that followed the army and executed troops that had retreated. In some areas, he placed Bolshevik "fence units" behind the army lines to shoot any retreating soldiers.

While all sides had committed crimes, it was generally due to a lack of discipline in the various bands rather than a policy of their leaders. Only the Bolshevik "Red Terror" was systematic and organized to eliminate a whole class of people, which included most officers.

When the White Army entered Ukraine, Trotsky convinced the Ukrainian nationalists that if the Whites — the remnants of the Russian army — should win, they would make Ukraine again part of the Russian Empire, while the Reds would grant it independence. But after the Ukrainian nationalists helped the Reds to defeat the White forces, Trotsky invited their leaders for a celebration and had them all shot.

Trotsky traveled from one rebellious area to another in an armored train equipped with cannons and carrying an armored car with a machine gun, and when the train came to a village that resisted the Bolsheviks, he bombarded it into submission and in some cases used poison gas.

The greatest resistance to the Bolsheviks was in the Cossack areas north of the Caucasian Mountains. Cossacks were descendants of runaway serfs who had settled on the southern edge of Russian territory and formed free, self-ruling communities that were in perpetual war with the native Muslim tribes, such as the Chechens. In return for being left autonomous, the Cossacks served as elite cavalry units in the Tsar's army. They spoke Ukrainian rather than Russian, and, because they owned their land, they worked hard, and their villages were more prosperous than in other areas of the country.

Obviously, the Bolsheviks could not tolerate an independent region of former elite troops, and in January 1919 the Bolshevik Party Central Committee passed a secret resolution on "de-Cossackization":

> In view of the experience of the civil war against the Cossacks, we must recognize as the only politically correct measure massive terror and a merciless fight against the rich Cossacks, who must be exterminated and physically disposed of, down to the last man.

In each village, revolutionary courts passed judgments on lists of suspects of "counterrevolutionary activity," and they were executed without delay. Whole villages were burned, and all males between eighteen and fifty were deported to the north for forced labor. All cattle and goods were seized and women, children and old people were forced to leave the area or were thrown into concentration camps. The head of the Ukrainian Cheka reported on such a camp:

> Gathered together in a camp near Maikop, the hostages, women, children and old men survive in the most appalling conditions, in the cold and the mud of October. They are dying like flies. The women will do anything to escape death. The soldiers guarding the camp take advantage of this and treat them as prostitutes.

It is estimated that between 1919 and 1920, out of the population of about three million, around 500,000 Cossacks were killed or died while being deported.

When in 1920 the remnants of the White Army were defeated on the Crimean peninsula, there were not enough ships to evacuate everyone, and only 150,000 people were able to escape to Turkey. After being assured that their lives would be spared, about 50,000 remaining soldiers and officers had surrendered. But once they laid down their arms, they were at the mercy of the Bolshevik Bela Kun and a female Cheka sadist Rozalia Zemliachka. The surrendered officers were tied to wooden planks and burned alive in locomotive furnaces, or were drowned in barges that were sunk at sea. The soldiers were hanged from the streetlamp posts, and for years to come the city of Sevastopol was known as "the city of the hanged."

THE NEW MORALITY

By 1921, the Cheka secret police grew to 200,000 agents, and their actions had caused even some of the more idealistic Communists to question their activities. One of them described the Cheka:

> This organization is rotten to the core: the canker of criminality, violence and totally arbitrary decisions abounds, and it is filled with common criminals and the dregs of society, men armed to the teeth who simply execute anyone they don't like. They steal, loot, rape, and throw anyone in prison, forge documents, practice extortion, and blackmail, and will let anyone go in exchange for huge sums of money.

In a report of October 16, 1919, an inspector from the headquarters wrote:

> Orgies and drunkenness are daily occurrences. Almost all the personnel of the Cheka are heavy cocaine users. They say that this helps them deal with the sight of so much blood on a daily basis. Drunk with blood and violence, the Cheka is

doing its duty, but it is made up of uncontrollable elements that will require close surveillance.

However, Dzerzhinsky, Trotsky, Stalin, and of course Lenin, dismissed these accusations. Lenin wrote that "(the Cheka) was unjustly accused of excesses by a few unrealistic intellectuals . . . incapable of considering the problem of terror in a wider perspective. A good Communist is a good Chekist."

Strange as it may seem, some Westerners also saw Lenin's terror in a "wider perspective." The Columbia University Professor Mark Lilla wrote in his book *The Reckless Mind:*

> Distinguished professors, gifted poets, and influential journalists summoned their talents to convince all who would listen that modern tyrants were liberators and that their unconscionable crimes were noble when seen in the right perspective.

In plain language, these professors believed that the ends of achieving the Communist Utopia justified the means of killing tens of millions of people. They surely had not included their own families among those to be sacrificed.

The newspaper of the Kiev Cheka justified the massacres as new idealism:

> We reject the old system of morality and humanity invented by the bourgeoisie . . . . Our morality has no precedence and our humanity is absolute because it rests on a new ideal. . . . To us, everything is permitted for we are the first to raise the sword not to oppress races and reduce

them to slavery, but to liberate humanity from its shackles ... Blood? Let blood flow like water! ... For only through the death of the old world can we liberate ourselves forever from the return of those jackals!

The Cambodian Communist Pol-Pot could not have said it better sixty years later.

In his book *The New Class,* the Yugoslav ex-Communist Milovan Djilas who had spent many years in Communist prisons, explained this "new morality":

No matter what your ideology may be, once you believe that you are in the possession of some infallible truth, you become a combatant in a religious war. There is nothing to prevent you from robbing, burning and slaughtering in the name of your truth, for you are doing it with a perfectly clear conscience — indeed, the truth in your possession makes it your duty to pursue it with an iron logic and unwavering will . . . ideology demands the liquidation of your enemies, real or imagined.

TODAY RUSSIA, TOMORROW THE WORLD

While the civil war was going on, the quest for world revolution was not being neglected. Karl Marx thought that because capitalism was worldwide, the revolution also had to be worldwide. He believed that world revolution would begin in a country with the most developed capitalism such as Germany because its working class would be the most socially conscious. He specifically did not think that this

country would be Russia. Lenin however was not going
to be distracted by such theoretical considerations and
insisted that it would be easier to have a revolution in a
country where capitalism was not yet sufficiently strong
to suppress it.

To spread the revolution throughout the world,
in 1919 Lenin established the Comintern (Communist
International), which would work "by all available
means, including armed force, for the overthrow of
the international bourgeoisie and for the creation of an
international Soviet Republic." By 1928 the Comintern
had 583,105 members all over the world, not counting the
Russians. Its chairman was a veteran associate of Lenin,
Grigori Zinoviev, whom Stalin had later executed.

As the civil war in Russia was being won, Lenin directed
his effort to duplicate the Russian revolution in Germany,
which meant to undermine the German Social Democratic
Republic. Here the Communists used the same tactics as in
Russia — disrupting meetings, organizing strikes and riots,
and later even joining the rising Nazi Storm Troopers in
joint actions against the government. Lenin believed that
if Germany became Communist, it would be easy to spread
the revolution to the ravaged-by-war France, England, and
other European countries.

The Communists competed with the Social Democrats
for votes of the working class and considered them bitterest
enemies because they advocated a gradual and peaceful
way to Socialism rather than revolution.

In his book *Out of the Night*, the former Comintern
agent Jan Valtin quotes one of its leaders:

> In order to deceive the masses, the Social
> Democrats deliberately proclaim that the chief
> enemy of the working class is Fascism. It is not

true that Fascism of the Hitler type represents the chief enemy.

In Valtin's opinion, if the Communists had joined the Social Democrats and voted against Hitler, he would not have come to power.

The German Communist Party launched an uprising against the Social Democrat government in Berlin, but it was quickly suppressed by the army and its leaders were shot. In April 1919, the Communists set up the Munich Commune that formed a Bavarian Red Army. They took over the banks and, like the Russian Communists, executed hostages. Similar disturbances were organized in other German cities.

In the summer of 1920, after the Red Army under Leon Trotsky defeated the Ukrainian and the Polish armies, Lenin ordered an attack on Warsaw, predicting that this "could be the Communization of all Europe before the new year." Trotsky's battle order was: "Heroes, let's take Warsaw! Just nine miles more and we will have all Europe ablaze."

The threat was real, and a French journalist reported:

> The perilous situation must be clearly understood. Warsaw is doomed. The Communist army of General Tukhachevsky will soon be joined by the dreaded cavalry of General Budenny, and this victorious force will enjoy a clear gallop to the Oder River. Germany not only is too weak to resist but within that country at least half the disgruntled population might be expected to rise in favor of the Russians. Within two weeks Tukhachevsky and Budenny could be on the border of France, and England must prepare itself for this dread

possibility. If the victorious Russians are able to enlist the support of the masses in one great revolutionary outburst, all Europe as we know it could be swept away.

Lenin was so sure that wherever the Red Army appeared, the peasants and workers would rise up and join the Communists, that he ordered a major part of General Tukhachevsky's force to be diverted into the German province of Pomerania to start a revolution there. But much to his dismay, the revolutions in Poland and Germany did not materialize, and the disorganized Polish army broke the Soviet communications code and routed the Red Army.

This was the second time in history that Poland had saved Europe. The first time was in 1683 when it defeated the Turks near Vienna.

Since the German revolution did not happen, Lenin's "plan B" was to prevent German cooperation with France and England. His hope was the possibility that in a future conflict they would weaken one another and could then be overwhelmed by the Soviet army. To realize this hope, Lenin and Trotsky decided that Germany should become powerful again. They established secret military cooperation with the German army to circumvent the restrictions of the Peace Treaty of Versailles that after World War I prohibited Germany from manufacturing and testing tanks, airplanes, submarines and poison gas. In return, the Germans instructed the Red Army in strategy and tactics. This cooperation lasted until Hitler came to power in 1933.

In October of 1918, Lenin sent the Hungarian Communist Bela Kun to Budapest to organize a Hungarian Communist Party. They were joined there by several hundred local Communists and established a "Republic of Soviets." Land and businesses were nationalized, and a terror group called "Lenin's Boys" traveled around the country requisitioning food from peasants and hanging those who resisted. The Republic lasted 133 days, during which they exchanged 218 messages with Lenin, who advised them to shoot Social Democrats. In his message of May 27, 1918, he explained:

> The dictatorship of the proletariat requires the use of swift, implacable and resolute violence to crush the resistance . . . Anyone who does not understand this is not a revolutionary.

When a right wing uprising defeated the Communists, Bella Kun escaped to Vienna where he was interned by the Social Democrat government that exchanged him for an Austrian prisoner held by Russia.

In most countries, the Comintern had set up secret prisons in which they tortured and killed their opponents, mostly Social Democrats, and from which they smuggled their kidnapped victims aboard Soviet ships to Russia. In the United States, the Comintern efforts were concentrated on gaining control of the maritime unions so that, by calling a strike on Lenin's orders, they could paralyze worldwide shipping. The American longshoremen union on the West Coast remained for a long time under Communist influence.

As Lenin wrote about the United States:

> The 'freer,' or more 'democratic,' a bourgeois country is, the more fiercely does the capitalist gang rage against worker's revolution; this is exemplified by the democratic republic of the United States of America. . . . No parliament can in any circumstances be for Communists an arena of struggle for reforms for the betterment

of the situation of the working class. . . . The only question can be that of utilizing bourgeois state institutions for their destruction.

In 1928, the presidential candidate of the American Communist Party, CPUSA, William Z. Foster, declared:

When a Communist heads a government in the United States — and that day will come just as surely as the sun rises — that government will not be a capitalist government, but a Soviet government, and behind the government will stand the Red Army to enforce the Dictatorship of the Proletariat.

When he ran again in 1932, he explained further:

Under the dictatorship, all the capitalist parties — Republican, Democratic, Progressive, Socialist, etc. — will be liquidated, the Communist party functioning alone as the party of the toiling masses. Likewise will be dissolved all other organizations that are political props of the bourgeois rule, including chambers of commerce, employer's associations, Rotary clubs, American Legion, Y.M.C.A., and such fraternal orders as the Masons, Odd Fellows, Elks, Knights of Columbus, etc. . . . The press, the motion picture, the radio, the theater, will be taken over by the government.

LENIN'S NEW ECONOMIC POLICY (NEP)

By the end of the Russian Civil War, about 15 million people were dead, 3 million of whom died of typhus and many more of starvation. In addition to the millions killed in the fighting, the Cheka murdered around 500,000

Cossacks, 250,000 political dissidents, many pacifist Mennonites who refused to be drafted, and about 100,000 Jews had perished in various pogroms. Also, the civil war had created about seven million street children, and about two million people had fled the country. The agricultural output dropped to one-third of that before the war and the industrial output to only one-seventh. *Pravda* reported:

> The workers of the towns and some of the villages choke in the throes of hunger. The railways barely crawl. The houses are crumbling. The towns are full of refuse. Epidemics spread and death strikes — industry is ruined.

Because in 1921 the food requisitioning squads in the provinces were still resisted with arms, the Red Army used airplane bombing and poison gas against the revolting villages and suppressed hunger marches in the cities with bullets.

Seeing that the situation was not improving, Lenin admitted that going directly to Communism at this stage was impractical, and announced a New Economic Policy, the NEP, which he called "temporary State Capitalism" and justified it as "making one step backward in order to make two steps forward later."

Under the NEP food requisitions ceased, and small farms and small businesses were returned to private ownership. After the peasants had paid their taxes by giving the government part of their products, they were permitted to sell the remainder at the going market prices, which gave them an incentive to produce more. Industry and transportation remained under government control.

But the NEP did not come in time to prevent the horrible famine of 1921 – 1922, when upward of 5 million people starved to death. The United States government had appropriated $20 million under the Russia Relief Act, and Herbert Hoover organized a massive relief program. He set up offices flying the Stars and Stripes in Ukraine and some other needy regions. The program was run by 300 Americans and 120,000 Russians, fed 10.5 million people daily, and its medical division helped fight the typhus epidemic. The program was halted in 1923 when it was discovered that the Soviets, while still receiving American grain, had secretly resumed selling their own grain abroad.

The political police, the Cheka, had penetrated every function of the country, and strict censorship was imposed on the press, radio, cinema, theater, and books, which were turned into instruments of state propaganda. Trade unions lost all power to bargain for higher wages, and functioned solely to make the workers produce more.

The minority nations of the Tsarist Empire, to which the Bolsheviks had promised independence, were brought into submission by the same means as the rest of Russia. The Caucasian region was divided into three Soviet Republics: Georgia, Armenia, and Azerbaijan, in which the terror was carried out by a twenty-five-year-old policeman named Lavrenti Beria, who in one week had 12,578 people shot.

In Central Asia, the native clans fought independently of one another and were no match for the Red Army, but some resistance continued in the mountains until the end of the 1920s. The area was later divided into five Soviet Republics: Turkmenistan, Uzbekistan, Tajikistan, Kazakhstan, and Kirgizia.

By 1922 the Bolsheviks controlled practically the whole country, and on December 28, the delegations of the Russian, Ukrainian, and Belarus republics signed the Union Treaty of 1922, that declared all of the Soviet Republics as one country: the Union of Soviet Socialist Republics or USSR.

LENIN'S DEATH

By the end of 1921, Lenin's health had deteriorated, and in March of 1922, Joseph Stalin was elected to take over as the Secretary General of the Communist Party. None of the other members of the seven-man Politburo that was running the country were interested in the job, which involved dealing with provincial party politicians and all kinds of paperwork. They considered themselves big revolutionary leaders and wanted to make big decisions. But Stalin knew what he was doing and began filling provincial positions with people who became beholden to him and who, when they become delegates to the periodic Party Congresses, would be electing the Party Presidium which in turn elected the seven members of the Politburo.

In May of 1922, Lenin had his first stroke which paralyzed his right side, and after suffering a second one in December, he was forced to stop working. Without Lenin to control them, the Politburo members went after one another. Unable to agree on a single leader, they settled on a trinity of Joseph Stalin, Grigory Zinoviev, and Lev Kamenev, Trotsky's brother-in-law. Stalin remained the Secretary General of the Party and also the Commissar of People's Inspection, which gave him the power to investigate anyone and anything he wished. Zinoviev remained the President of the Komintern, and Kamenev took over Lenin's second position that was the equivalent of prime minister.

Trotsky, who had believed that he was second only to Lenin, felt sidetracked and began campaigning against the Trinity. But because of his arrogant personality he was widely disliked and was opposed by the other Politburo members, who were continually making alliances against each other.

CHAPTER 4
WHO WAS STALIN?

Joseph Stalin, whose real surname was Jughashvili, was born in 1879 in the small Georgian town of Gori. As a boy he had smallpox, which left him with pockmarks all over his face, and at twelve, he was run over by a carriage and his left arm was shorter than the right. His father was a shoemaker, and Joseph was given a choice of becoming either a shoemaker's apprentice or, as his mother had insisted, to go to a seminary to train for the priesthood in the Georgian Church. Like Karl Marx and Vladimir Lenin, he was arrogant and rude.

While at the seminary, Joseph began reading Marxist literature and wrote poetry in Georgian. In 1898, he became involved with Russian Marxists who had been exiled to Georgia, and helped to organize a strike of tram workers for which he was arrested but was quickly released. In 1899, he was expelled from the seminary for not showing up for an exam. In 1903, he was exiled to a village in Siberia, but immediately escaped and returned to Georgia, where he was hidden by one of the exiled revolutionaries, Lev Kamenev, whom he will have executed in the 1930s. His quick return from Siberia made him suspect of cooperating with the police, but he soon became one of the leaders of the Caucasian Social Democrat party (before it split into Bolsheviks and Mensheviks), and began using the name

Koba, taken from a Georgian Robin Hood-type legend. In 1905, Stalin went to a meeting in Finland where he met Lenin and upon returning to Georgia proclaimed himself the Lenin of the Caucasus, which gave him authority.

He married his pregnant girlfriend Kato, most of whose family he would in the 1930s send to the Gulag or exterminate. In 1907, his wife died and their son, named Yakov, was given to his wife's sister. Stalin did not ask about his son Yakov for fourteen years, and during World War II refused to trade a captured German general for the captured-by-the-Germans Yakov, who died in captivity. Stalin's relationship with his mother was not much better: after he left Georgia, he visited her only three times and did not come to her funeral. When on one of the visits she asked him what was it that he actually did, he explained that he was sort of like the Tsar, to which she replied that she still wished he had become a priest.

In 1907, Stalin organized a bank robbery during which about forty people were killed or maimed by a hand grenade, and in 1908 he was recaptured and sentenced to three years in a village in Northern Russia. He escaped in 1909 but was captured again and was sent back to a distant village, this time for five years. While there, he was able to correspond with other Bolsheviks (and was elected a member of the Central Committee), learned German, used a library, and in 1912 was instrumental in setting up the newspaper *Pravda*. Later that year he escaped to Europe, disguised as a woman.

Upon his return, he was rearrested and sent to a village near the Arctic Circle. Here he lived with a family and seduced their thirteen-year-old daughter who bore a girl, whom he never acknowledged as his. Between 1902 and 1913, Stalin was arrested eight times, exiled seven times and escaped six times. The escapes must have taught him that this was no way to handle one's enemies, and that a bullet in the back of the head would be much more effective.

LENIN'S TESTAMENT

Lenin was suspicious of Stalin, and fearing a split in the party upon his death, wrote on December 25, 1922, in his Testament:

> Comrade Stalin, having become Secretary-General has unlimited authority concentrated in his hands, and I am not sure whether he will always be capable of using this authority with sufficient caution. Comrade Trotsky . . . is distinguished not only by outstanding ability. . . . He is personally perhaps the most capable man in the present Central Committee, but he has displayed excessive self-assurance. . . . These two qualities of the two outstanding leaders of the present Central Committee can inadvertently lead to a split, and if our party does not take steps to avert this, the split may come unexpectedly.

On January 4, 1923, Lenin added a postscript:

> Stalin is too rude and this defect, although quite tolerable in our midst and in dealing among us Communists, becomes intolerable in a Secretary-General. This is why I suggest that the comrades think about a way of removing Stalin from that post and appointing another man in his stead.

This postscript may have been caused by complaints from Lenin's wife, Nadezhda, that Stalin had been rude to her, and on March 5, Lenin wrote to Stalin announcing the severance of all "personal and comradely relations." But soon afterward Lenin had his third stroke and died on January 20, 1924. After Lenin's death, his Testament conveniently disappeared.

Stalin knew that Lenin was dying, and to get Trotsky out of the way, convinced him to take a vacation in the Caucasus. Then, with Trotsky not around, as soon as Lenin died, Stalin made a dramatic speech before the Congress of the Soviets implying that Lenin had made him his successor:

> Departing from us, Comrade Lenin bequeathed to us the duty of guarding and strengthening the dictatorship of the proletariat. We vow to you, Comrade Lenin, that we will spare no effort to fulfill also this bequest of yours with honor.
>
> Lenin never regarded the Republic of Soviets as an end in itself. He always regarded it as a necessary link for strengthening the revolutionary movements in the lands of the West and the East. . . . We vow to you Comrade Lenin that we will not spare our lives to strengthen and expand the union of the toilers of the whole world, the Communist International.

He went on like this for a long time with a list of presumably Lenin's bequests.

HOW STALIN BECAME A DICTATOR

While Stalin's position was strong, it was not completely secure. The most dangerous moment for him happened in May 1924 when at a meeting of the Central Committee, Lenin's widow Nadezhda Krupskaya insisted that Lenin's Testament, including the postscript that called for Stalin's removal from the post of Secretary General, should be read at the approaching Congress of the party. If a four to three majority of the seven members of Politburo (Stalin, Trotsky, Zinoviev, Kamenev, Rykov, Bukharin, and Tomsky) had supported this, Stalin could have been removed.

But after Lenin's death, the members of the Politburo feared that if Stalin were removed, his successor would be the quarrelsome and arrogant Trotsky, whom all of them intensely disliked. This is why Stalin's position was saved by Zinoviev, who declared that, happily, Lenin's fears about Stalin had proved unfounded, and by Kamenev, who urged that Lenin's Testament should remain secret. Being saved by them did not stop Stalin from having all six Politburo members executed. In the 1930s, Zinoviev, Kamenev, Rykov, and Bukharin were shot; Tomsky, anticipating what was coming, shot himself, and Trotsky was later assassinated by a Soviet agent in Mexico.

In his capacity as Secretary General, Stalin had the power to appoint provincial functionaries, and kept postponing the next Party Congress until he was sure that the majority of delegates would vote for him.

Seeing Stalin's power grow, in 1926 the Politburo members Zinoviev and Kamenev joined Trotsky in accusing Stalin of trying to establish a one-man rule, but Bukharin, Rykov, and Tomsky supported Stalin. With a four to three majority in his favor, Stalin prevailed.

Trotsky's theory of "Permanent Revolution" stated that, as taught by Karl Marx, for the revolution to succeed it has to be worldwide. But Stalin claimed that his theory of socialism in one country had been formulated by Lenin, and that he was just interpreting it. Once Stalin accused his opponents of being anti-Lenin, no one dared to support them; and when the Party Congress, full of Stalin's supporters, finally met, it approved Stalin's position. Trotsky, Zinoviev, and Kamenev were dubbed the "left opposition," driven out of the Politburo, and in 1927 expelled from the Party. Their places in the Politburo were given to Stalin's followers, giving him a permanent four to three majority and absolute power.

Once the left opposition had been silenced, Stalin did not need his former allies Bukharin, Rykov and Tomsky any longer, and because they advocated the continuation of the New Economic Policy which Stalin wanted to end, he called them the "right opposition." And, since no one dared to support them, Stalin became unopposed and an absolute dictator.

While the New Economic Policy had given the country a breathing spell (grain production had doubled, and peasants flooded the local markets with produce), Stalin wanted to do something on a grand scale that would be identified with him, much as the Revolution was identified with Lenin. Such action would be the forcing of all peasants into collective farms that would affect 120 million people living in 600,000 villages.

In 1926, the dreaded head of the Cheka, Felix Dzerzhinsky, died. In Poland, it was gleefully said that the Communist Dzerzhinsky had killed more Russians than the anti-Communist Polish president Josef Pilsudski, whose army had defeated the Soviets in 1920. Dzerzhinsky's successor was another former Polish aristocrat, Vyacheslav Menzhinsky, who had headed the United States department of the Cheka, which was now renamed GPU (Governmental Political Directorate).

Menzhinsky had been a lawyer and a professor of history and like Stalin and Dzerzhinsky wrote poetry. He wore a three-piece suit and a bowler hat and had traveled widely abroad, including in the United States. While in Paris, he had worked as a bank clerk, which is why during the revolution he was appointed the first Commissar of Finance.

It was the Menzhinsky's GPU that in 1928 forced peasants into collective farms and executed or exiled to Siberia those who resisted. But Menzhinsky was in poor health, and frequently interrogated prisoners while laying down and covered by a blanket. Because of that, he depended heavily on his aide and future successor Genrikh Yagoda. Menzhinsky died in 1934 under suspicious circumstances, possibly poisoned by Yagoda, who had been a pharmacist and knew all about poisons.

Chapter 5
What Was Collectivization?

Collectivization was Stalin's policy to force peasants into collective farms, called kolkhozes. They had to surrender not only the land they had received after the revolution but also the land their families had owned for generations. Their fields, horses, wagons, agricultural implements, and farm animals became the property of the kolkhoz. Now, the formerly independent farmers had to do what they were told by someone who became their boss not because he was a better farmer, but only because he had joined the Communist Party. The only way they could show their disapproval was to slaughter their cattle rather than surrender it to the kolkhoz. In 1930 alone, out of a total of 70 million heads of cattle 14 million were killed, as were a third of all pigs and a quarter of all sheep and goats.

The poorest peasants, who had no land or animals to lose, welcomed the opportunity to use someone else's property and cooperated with the authorities. Some became members of the Communist Party and were appointed to manage the kolkhozes. But they were the least knowledgeable farmers, the least energetic, and the ones most inclined to imbibing.

The better-off peasants who refused to give up their farms, were called "kulaks" and declared to be "enemies of the people." A kulak was defined as a peasant who employed hired labor or who owned power-driven machinery. In 1928, Stalin declared that: "We have gone from limiting the exploiting tendencies of the kulak to a policy of liquidating the kulak as a class." In Ukraine alone, 33,000 "kulak" families were evicted and deported to Siberia or Kazakhstan. Many died of hunger or cold during the weeks-long trips in cattle cars, and any resistance was brutally suppressed by the GPU.

The collectivization was a gigantic operation by the Communist Party and the GPU secret police. To prevent peasants from escaping to the cities, photo-identifications called the "internal passports" were issued to city dwellers but not to peasants. Without such a passport, one could not get a job or a police permit to move into a town. Because of this, peasants could not leave the collective farms just as before in 1861, when they were still serfs, they could not leave their landlords.

In the kolkhoses, the peasants were assigned to work brigades and, according to the amount of work they performed, were credited with units called "workdays." After the harvest, part of the grain was delivered to the government and whatever was left was divided by the total number of workdays. Then the peasants received their share according to the workdays they had accumulated. A day of skilled work, like driving a tractor, merited more than one "workday."

This method of requisitioning grain from the collective granaries was so effective that during World War II when the Germans occupied part of the Soviet Union, they kept the collective farm system.

With deportation of the kulaks, who were the most productive peasants, grain deliveries decreased and many peasants were accused of sabotage — of refusing to harvest or of pilfering grain. In 1932, a decree in Stalin's handwriting ordered death by shooting or ten years of imprisonment for stealing state property, which became known as the "five stalks law" because a handful of grain stalks was considered state property. Under this law, in just one region of Ukraine, 1,500 death sentences were passed in one month.

From 1930 to 1931, 1,803,392 men, women and children were deported as part of de-kulakization. But in January of 1932, when the authorities conducted the census, only 1,317,022 were recorded, i.e., about half a million people were missing. The statistician who had released these figures was shot for disclosing the government secret that the missing 500,000 were dead.

In the winter of 1932 – 1933 people again began to die of starvation. While there were large reserves of grain in local granaries, and in 1932, two million metric tons were exported, the reserves were not allowed to be used to feed the starving. Also, the GPU surrounded Ukraine and did not allow grain to be brought in from outside. In his book *I Chose Freedom,* a Soviet defector, Victor Kravchenko, quoted the explanation given to him by an official:

> A ruthless struggle is going on between the peasantry and our regime. It's a struggle to the death. This year was a test of our strength and their endurance. It took a famine to show them who is master here. It has cost millions of lives, but the collective farm system is here to stay.

During these two years, about 8 million people starved to death: more than 6 million in Ukraine, 1 million in the Cossack area of Northern Caucasus, and 1 million in Kazakhstan. There was rampant cannibalism. Peasants brought their children into towns and abandoned them in the hope that someone would feed them. Corpses were lying on the sides of the roads, and I remember hearing my mother saying that every day she saw horse wagons carrying them away, stacked like cord-wood. In the Ukrainian city of Kharkov alone, the death rate rose from 9,000 in June 1932, to 100,000 in June 1933. Also, during these two years, there were about 15,000 riots and peasant revolts, all brutally suppressed by the GPU.

One of the participants in the atrocities, the writer Lev Kopelev, explained in his book *The Education of a True Believer,* his reasoning when, as a member of a GPU team he took part in the forced requisitioning of food from peasants. He wrote that he had been forever haunted by the memories of an old man and a boy in whose hut the team noticed that a section of its clay floor appeared to have been recently refinished, and dug up from it several sacks of grain. The crying old man fell to his knees and begged them to leave at least some of the grain or both of them would starve. They took everything. Kopelev wrote:

> It was excruciating to see and hear all this. And even worse to take part in it . . . I persuaded myself, explained to myself, I must not give in to debilitating pity. We were realizing historical necessity. We were performing our revolutionary duty. We were obtaining grain for the socialist fatherland. . . . With the others, I emptied out the old folks' storage chests, stopping my ears to the children's crying.

> ... I saw all this and did not go out of my mind.
> Nor did I curse those who had sent me to take
> away the peasants' grain in the winter. . . . Nor
> did I lose my faith. As before, I believed because
> I wanted to believe.

But not a word about the famine appeared in the Soviet press. When rumors of it reached the West, they were denied, and unlike during the previous famine, no foreign relief was accepted. Instead, a guided tour of Ukraine was conducted with *The New York Times* correspondent Walter Duranty, who received the 1932 Pulitzer Prize for his reports that there was no famine in Ukraine. (*The New York Times* later acknowledged that these articles denying the famine were "some of the worst reporting to appear in this newspaper.")

In his memoir *Khrushchev Remembers*, the former Soviet dictator Nikita Khrushchev wrote about the de-kulakization: "I can't give an exact figure because no one was keeping it. All we knew was that people were dying in enormous numbers."

After Stalin abolished the NEP and living conditions deteriorated again, he needed a scapegoat, and by the end of 1928 thousands of Soviet managers and engineers were accused of industrial sabotage, right-wing deviation, or belonging to a "socially alien class." Between January 1930 and June 1931, 48 percent of engineers in the Donbass coal mining region were dismissed or arrested, having been accused of sabotage of the five-year plan, of causing industrial accidents or of damaging equipment, particularly if it was imported and for which there were no spare parts available.

In September of 1930, Stalin issued instructions to the Chairman of the Council of People's Commissars Vyacheslav Molotov:

> It is imperative to (1) carry out a radical purge of the whole of the People's Commissariat of Finance and the state Bank. . . (2) shoot at least twenty or thirty of the saboteurs who managed to infiltrate these organizations . . . (3) step up GPU operations all over the country to recover all silver coins that are still in circulation.

Several weeks later, *Pravda* published the confessions of forty-eight members of the Finance Commissariat who accepted responsibility for "the difficulties currently being experienced in the supply of food and for the sudden disappearance of silver coins." All forty-eight were executed three days later.

The secret police suspected former small business owners of hoarding Tsarist gold coins. They jailed the oldest men in their families and held them until their relatives brought some gold coins. This was called "sitting for gold." Those who did not have gold coins had to buy them, which was dangerous to both the buyer and the seller, because it was a criminal offense for the seller not to have surrendered them to the government. I remember overhearing my parents talking about how the old men were given only herring to eat, and were not given any water. Many of the old men did not survive.

On November 9, 1932, Stalin's wife, Nadezhda Alliluyeva, committed suicide. In her memoir, *Only One Year,* Stalin's daughter Svetlana (who had left the Soviet Union in 1966), described the aftermath:

They (her aunts) told me that the event had so shaken everyone that people lost their heads, thinking of how best to conceal what had happened. For that reason doctors had not been permitted to examine the body, there had been no medical verdict, the obituaries had mysteriously spoken of an 'unexpected death'.

The wife of Politburo member Nikolai Bukharin, a friend of Stalin's wife, wrote in her book *This I Cannot Forget*, what her husband told her what had happened the night before:

(He) had seen her in the Kremlin at a banquet in honor of the October Revolution. According to him, Stalin, half-drunk, had thrown cigarette butts and orange peels in his wife's face. Unable to bear such humiliation, she had got up and left before the end of the dinner. The following morning (she) was found dead. Supposedly she had shot herself, although the state press would report to the public that she died of peritonitis.

STALIN'S FIVE-YEAR PLANS

In April of 1929, Stalin announced the first five-year plan of industrialization. It called for a 230% increase in industrial production, doubling the output of oil and coal, and tripling the output of iron and steel. Almost immediately after the announcement, Stalin demanded that it be fulfilled in four years instead of five. I remember that when I had finished eating my porridge, the call for fulfilling the five-year plan in four years stared at me from the bottom of the bowl, the rim of which was decorated with tractors and harvesters.

In August of 1929, the days of the week were abolished, and there were no more Saturdays and Sundays — only five workdays and one day of rest. This remained in force until someone figured out that by working six days and having the seventh day off, there would be more working days, and the old calendar was restored.

While the five-year plan was adopted in mid-1929, in January 1933 it was backdated to October of 1928, and it was declared that thanks to Stalin's great leadership it had actually been fulfilled in four years.

An Oxford scholar, Ronald Hindley, described the situation as follows:

> Forever publicizing percentages and tonnages to what allegedly had been, was being, should be, could be, might have been produced in the way of coal, oil, pig-iron, steel, tractors, combine harvesters, factories, hydroelectric stations and the like, Stalin invested an air of spurious exactitude pronouncements essentially magical and liturgical.

Both major newspapers the *Pravda* (*The Truth*) and *Izvestia* (*The News*) were full of glowing reports of fulfillment and over-fulfillment of the plan, to which no one paid any attention, because it was no secret that in *The Truth* there was no news, and in *The News*, there was no truth.

To stimulate production during the second five-year plan, government propagandists needed an example of a dedicated worker, and picked a coal miner named Andrei Stakhanov who had presumably over-fulfilled his production norm fourteen-fold. They did not mention that he did it with several helpers. Stakhanov became a "Hero of Socialist Labor," awarded all sorts of medals, appeared in newsreels, and became a delegate to the Soviet of People's Deputies. Not used to being a celebrity and having money, he soon drank himself to death.

But his name became a symbol of a socialist shock worker and was supposed to inspire "socialist competition." Every factory and office now had to have its own Stakhanovites, with their pictures displayed on bulletin boards. To determine who had over-fulfilled their quotas for every task, the quotas had to be created in a hurry. Even children found this situation ridiculous, and a ditty began secretly circulating among them:

> They've issued a new program, to shit no less than a kilogram.
>
> Those who seven can afford will receive a nice reward.
>
> Those who only do a pound will be beaten to the ground.

The problem with these quotas was that they measured only quantity and disregarded quality, so that a factory making shoes would be praised for high production even if no one wanted to buy them because they were falling apart in only a few months.

CHAPTER 6
THE GULAG

The word GULAG is an abbreviation for the Russian title Main Administration of Camps, but everyone understood that the acronym stood for the slave labor system that the writer Alexander Solzhenitsyn called *The Gulag Archipelago*. In 1918, Lenin demanded that "unreliable elements such as aristocrats, merchants, policemen, officers, clergy, and others, be locked up in concentration camps outside major towns" and by 1921, there were eighty-four such camps.

In 1929, Stalin decided that forced labor was essential for the achievement of his five-year plans, and gave control of the camps to the secret police. Their network was expanded throughout the country and grew to 476 camp complexes with thousands of sub-camps, each containing from a few thousand to many thousands of prisoners. By 1939 an estimated 5 million prisoners worked in logging, mining, construction, factories, farming, and even scientific laboratories.

The mass arrests of 1937 and 1938 rapidly filled the camps, and as the American writer Anne Applebaum wrote in her book *Gulag*:

Never in the history of the world literature could the writers have seen anything like this:

mass extermination of people who did not know why they were being killed after the last drop of strength had been squeezed out of them.

When the Gulag became full and no more prisoners were needed, hundreds of thousands of the newly arrested were shot in the back of the head while standing on the edge of ditches they themselves had been forced to dig. After the collapse of the Soviet Union, one of the executioners interviewed on television whined how his trigger finger had hurt from shooting prisoners all day long with a pistol. He was asking for sympathy.

THE TERROR YEARS 1937 – 1938

An atmosphere of fear hung over the country. In many towns, columns of Gulag prisoners in shabby gray quilted uniforms, from which dirty white cotton oozed out in torn places, were escorted by NKVD (the new name for the OGPU) guards with German Shepherds or driven in open trucks to construction sites. But the number of the Gulag's victims was not limited to the prisoners who were there at any particular time. Their wives, children, siblings, parents, and grandparents raised the number of affected people to tens of millions, and set a nightmarish tone in the whole country.

In her book *Hope Against Hope,* Nadezhda Mandelshtam, whose husband had perished in the Gulag, wrote:

We never asked on hearing about the latest arrest, 'What was he arrested for?' but we were exceptional. Most people, crazed by fear, asked this question just to give themselves a little hope; if others were arrested for some reason, then they would not be arrested, because they had not done anything wrong . . . (They could not) understand that people were arrested for nothing.

Who then were the people suspected of being dangerous to the state and whom Stalin feared? There were several groups:

1. The Old Bolsheviks, the dedicated revolutionaries who had risked their lives to create the Soviet System but might have had ideas of their own, and just as they had revolted against the Tsar, could possibly organize a revolt against Stalin.

2. The foreign born — Poles, Moldovans, Germans, Koreans, etc. Between July 1937 and November 1938, there were 335,513 people of foreign origin arrested and most were executed. Even of the 394 foreign Communist members of the Comintern Executive Committee in 1936, only 171 remained in 1937.

3. Anyone who had communicated with foreign countries was suspected of being a spy even if he had corresponded with relatives or with foreigners with common interests, such as Esperanto clubs, stamp collectors, coin collectors, etc.

4. Priests, ministers, rabbis, and people who held religious services in secret or who had defended religion in general.

5. Nationalists (other than Russians, of course), who promoted their ethnic cultures.

6. Anyone who was critical of the Soviet system or its leaders, or might have told a joke that could be so interpreted.

7. Those needed to meet the regional quotas of arrests, some set personally by Stalin without specifying causes or

names, apparently just to terrorize the general population. For example, the July 30, 1937, quota for the Belorussian Republic was 12,000 – 2,000 to be executed and 10,000 sentenced to Gulag for eight to ten years. It was left to the local NKVD to find the appropriate victims, which created a form of "socialist competition" of productivity between the regional NKVDs and had developed a life of its own. It was dangerous for the local NKVD to have found fewer spies, saboteurs, and other enemies than were caught in a neighboring region — they could be accused of inadequate vigilance and themselves wind up in the Gulag.

AFTER THE ARREST

When the arrested were brought to a prison, they were registered, photographed and fingerprinted. They were not told why they were arrested, and for the first few days did not encounter any officials. As reported by Anne Applebaum, Inna Geister, arrested for being the daughter of an enemy of the people, described her first hours in the Lubianka prison in Moscow:

> Here, in Lubianka, you are already not a person. And around you, there are no people. They lead you down the corridor, photograph you, undress you, search you mechanically. Everything is done completely impersonally. You look for a human glance — I don't speak of a human voice, just a human glance — but you don't find it. You stand disheveled in front of the photographer, try somehow to fix your clothes, and are shown with a finger where to sit, an empty voice says 'face front' and 'profile.' They don't see you as a human being! You have become an object.

The next step was the interrogation, the objective of which was not only to get a signed confession to a fictitious transgression but also to obtain a list of presumed accomplices. Guilt or innocence had nothing to do with it. Torture became an official policy: Stalin sent a memo to the regional NKVDs confirming that "from 1937 on, in NKVD practice the use of physical pressure was permitted by the Central Committee."

To convince the population that the accused prominent Communists whom Stalin wanted to liquidate were actually enemies of Communism, he ordered Show Trials. The less-known victims were lumped together by categories, and the whole lists were sentenced by the infamous troikas, usually consisting of the head of the regional NKVD, the Regional Party Secretary, and the representative of the local prosecutor's office. They never saw the accused, but since they already had their signed confessions, there was no need to see them. In 1938, when Khrushchev became the Party Secretary of Ukraine, he was part of the troika that sentenced 54,000 people to death.

Evgenia Ginzburg, a former party member, accused of belonging to a "counter-revolutionary Trotskyite group" and sentenced to ten years, the first two of which she spent mostly in solitary confinement, wrote in her book *Journey Into the Whirlwind:*

> The daily routine in the Lubianka prison: at six in the morning a guard shouted 'prepare for the toilet!' and the women would silently line up in pairs. They were given ten minutes to use it, to wash up, and to wash their clothes... Before lunch of prison soup of grain or rotten cabbage, a twenty minutes walk in a small enclosed yard — single file next to the wall; then the same soup for dinner

and another walk to the toilet in the evening. . .
In every cell there was at least one informer, and
when there were only two people in the cell, each
suspected the other. A new prisoner in the cell
was always suspected and was ostracized, and
there was no criticism of the Soviet regime.

Usually, the prisons were used only for temporary
confinement. Then came the transport to the Gulags,
which in larger cities began by being transported to the
railroad station in closed trucks nicknamed "Black Ravens,"
that had the word "bread" or "vegetables" painted on their
sides. Then came the train. An American prisoner, Thomas
Sgovio, describes the horror: "Our train left Moscow on the
evening of June 24th. It was the beginning of an eastwards
journey which was to last a month. I can never forget the
moment . . . seventy men began to cry."

There were two kinds of railroad cars. Some were
regular third class cars modified by making the partitions
between compartments out of steel mesh, and those
between compartments and the corridor out of steel bars,
so that a guard could see inside and control the prisoners.
Guards also decided when to take the prisoners to the toilet,
usually once or twice a day, which created big problems for
people who could not hold out. The other kind of car was
the common cattle car that sometimes did not have bunks
and people were packed like sardines. But, the advantage
of the cattle cars was a hole in the floor that the prisoners
could use at any time as a toilet.

The food in transport usually consisted of bread and
salted fish, which created a problem of its own, because
the prisoners were usually getting only one cup of water
a day, and sometimes not even that. One prisoner wrote:
"Once, for three days we did not get water, and on New

Year's Eve of 1939, somewhere near Lake Baykal, we had to lick the black icicles which hung from the train carriages." Another prisoner wrote: "In a twenty-eight-day trip, we were given water three times, with the train occasionally stopping to take the corpses off."

Alexander Solzhenitsyn, in his book *The Gulag Archipelago,* tried to put himself into the minds of the guards:

> Here they were, understaffed, and then to have to carry water in pails — it had to be hauled a long way too, and it is insulting: why should a Soviet soldier have to carry water like a donkey for enemies of the people? But the convoys could have born with all that, hauled the water, and doled it out, if only those pigs, after slurping up the water, did not ask to go to the toilet.

The prisoners sentenced to the Gulag in the gold mines of the Kolyma peninsula in Siberia were unloaded in the transit camps on the Pacific coast to wait for ships, but there were not enough barracks. One prisoner who had arrived there in 1947 wrote: "Under the open sky they kept 20,000 people . . . they sat down and lived there on the ground. . . . The food was still only salted fish and bread, and the water situation did not improve."

Another prisoner wrote:

> All over the camp signs were posted. 'Do not drink unboiled water.' And two epidemics were raging among us — typhus and dysentery. And the prisoners did not heed the signs and drank water which trickled here and there on the grounds of the compound . . . Anyone can understand how desperate we became for a drink of water.

Some of the women prisoners resorted to prostitution, and some who did not were gang-raped by criminal prisoners.

When the old freighters with letters "DS" on their smoke stacks, signifying Far-Eastern Construction "Dalstroy", arrived, they had machine gun nests on their decks and their holds were divided into sections for 100 people each. When the ship passed near Japan, the prisoners were kept below deck so they would not be seen by Japanese fishermen. Food was thrown down into the hold and water was lowered in buckets so that prisoners had to fight for it. When in 1939 one of these ships carrying 1,500 inmates hit a reef near the Japanese island of Hokkaido, the crew let them drown, rather than seek assistance.

Evgenia Ginzburg wrote:

> If I remained on my feet it was only because there was no room to fall . . . It was impossible to move, our legs grew numb, hunger and the sea made us dizzy, and all of us were seasick . . . packed tightly in our hundreds we could hardly breathe, we sat or lay on the dirty floor or on one another, spreading our legs to make room for the person in front.

When the ship finally docked at the Gulag camp, the prisoners were greeted by banners hung on plywood boards above the entrance: "LABOR IN THE USSR IS A MATTER OF HONESTY, GLORY, VALOR, AND HEROISM!" or "WITH JUST WORK, I WILL PAY MY DEBT TO THE FATHERLAND." Others proclaimed the intent of the Soviet system: **"WITH AN IRON FIST, WE WILL LEAD HUMANITY TO HAPPINESS!"** or the rather familiar one: "THROUGH LABOR – FREEDOM!" – the same as the Nazis had placed over the gate of their worst concentration camp, Auschwitz: "Arbeit Macht Frei!"

The incoming prisoners were stripped, washed and shaved of all body hair. In some camps they were allowed to wear their own clothes that had been deloused by baking in special ovens; in others, they were not, and were issued camp uniforms that were frequently ragged, without regard to size.

Then came the most critical procedure that determined the fate of the prisoners: selection for work assignment, based on the prisoner's ability to work.

The camps were surrounded by several rings of barbed wire, with a space in between where the soil was raked so that it would show any footprints. Attack dogs roamed between the fences, and any prisoner coming within fifteen feet of the fence into the "no man's land", the forbidden death zone, could be shot by the guards without warning.

To stimulate productivity, the work columns in some larger camps departed every morning to the sound of patriotic music played by prisoner-musicians who, after the columns passed, put away their instruments and had to run to join their column.

The work day varied from eight to twelve hours, with two ten-minute breaks and a half hour for lunch. However, when the quota had not been fulfilled, prisoners frequently had to work as long as it took to fulfill it. The barracks were either wooden shacks or earth dugouts, infested by lice and bed bugs, and while bathing and delousing was prescribed every ten days, in practice it could be once in two months. Clothing was deloused by boiling or baking, and the prisoners did not always get their own clothing back, which led to fights.

Food also varied from camp to camp — in some, prisoners got watery soup of cabbage and potatoes once a day, in others, twice. How much bread a prisoner received depended on the fulfillment of work quotas; those who did not make the quota received a smaller ration. Less bread made them weaker the next day, and since their performance could not improve, they received even less, which soon led to starvation.

Sometimes, the food froze or didn't arrive for several days, and when bread finally did arrive there was another challenge. Ann Applebaum quotes a writer friend of Solzhenitsyn, Dmitri Panin, who wrote:

> When you get your ration you have an overwhelming desire to stretch the pleasure of eating it, cutting your bread up evenly into tiny pieces, rolling the crumbs into little balls. From sticks and strings, you improvise a pair of scales and weigh every piece. In such ways, you try to prolong the business of eating by three hours or more. But this is tantamount to suicide! Never on any account take more than a half-hour to consume your ration. Every bite of bread should be chewed thoroughly, to enable the stomach to digest it as easily as possible so that it give up to one's organism a maximum amount of energy ... if you always split your ration and put aside a part of it for the evening, you are finished. Eat it all at one sitting; if on the other hand, you gobble it down too quickly, as famished people often do in normal circumstances, you will also shorten your days.

Survival also depended on the brigadier — the prisoner in charge of the work brigade. He could be trying to improve his own situation at the expense of others, or he could be a comrade trying to do the best under the circumstances.

The work quotas were very detailed: a certain number of cubic meters of wood to be cut down, of ditches to be dug, of coal to be hauled. Different quotas were assigned to shoveling snow depending on whether it was freshly fallen light snow, lightly packed snow, heavily packed snow, or frozen snow. It was a serious business — food rations, which means survival, depended on their fulfillment.

As to how many people died in the Gulag is difficult, if not impossible to calculate. Anne Applebaum wrote:

> A number based on archival sources is available, although even the historian who compiled it points out that it is incomplete, and does not cover all categories of prisoners in every year: 2,749,163. . . . Yet even this number — which, in my view, is too precise to be reliable — still does not include those who died on the trains to the camps, those who died during interrogation; those whose executions were not technically "political" but were nevertheless carried out on spurious grounds; the more than 20,000 Polish officers who died in the Katyn massacres; and most of all those who died within a few days of release.

After Stalin's death, his successors began dismantling the Gulag, but it did not disappear altogether. In the 1970s and early 1980s some camps were redesigned for other dissidents such as anti-Soviet nationalist separatists who wanted their republics to secede from the Soviet Union, Jewish refuseniks who were not allowed to emigrate, and for criminals. Even in the 1980s, President Reagan and

Gorbachev were discussing the Soviet camps, and only in 1987 did Mikhail Gorbachev, the last ruler of the Soviet Union, himself a grandson of a Gulag prisoner, dissolve them completely.

In her book *Gulag*, Anne Applebaum raises the question of why the Western countries seemed indifferent to the Soviet terrors, why no one knew, for example, about "the terror famine of the 1930s in which Stalin killed more Ukrainians than Hitler murdered Jews. . . . How many in the West remember it?" And the writer Arthur Koestler wrote that most Western intellectuals would be embarrassed if they did not know the name of some writer or artist, but not that they did not know about millions of their fellow humans living in slavery.

Only the trade unions such as the American Federation of Labor, had supported boycott of Soviet goods and the Tariff Act of 1930 which stated that "All goods . . . mined, produced or manufactured . . . by convict labor or/and forced labor . . . shall not be entitled to entry at any of the ports of the United States."

CHAPTER 7
WHO KILLED KIROV?

On December 1, 1934, Sergei Kirov, the head of the Communist Party in the city of Leningrad, was assassinated. He had been popular with many party members, and in the election of the Party Central Committee in 1933, out of 1,966 votes, there were only three against Kirov, but 270 votes against Stalin. This enraged Stalin, who insisted that only three votes should be registered against him also.

Since Kirov's popularity created the possibility that at the next Party Congress he might compete with Stalin for the post of First Secretary, his assassination raised a suspicion that Stalin might have had something to do with it. Also, according to Khrushchev, because Stalin did not know who had voted against him, he later had 1,108 of the delegates shot, as well as ninety-eight of the 139 members of the Party Central Committee.

In his secret speech in 1956, Nikita Khrushchev, who followed Stalin as the First Secretary of the party, said:

> It must be asserted that to this day the circumstances that surrounded Kirov's murder hide many things that are inexplicable.... After the murder, top functionaries of the Leningrad NKVD were given very light sentences, but in 1937 they were shot. We can assume that they were

shot in order to cover the traces of the organizers of Kirov's killing.

And in his memoir published in 1989, Khrushchev wrote: "I believe that the murder was organized by Yagoda (head of the NKVD), who could have taken this action only on secret instructions from Stalin, received face to face."

The assassin, a disgruntled former party functionary named Leonid Nikolaev, was able to enter the party building because for some unexplained reason the NKVD guards had been withdrawn. Nikolaev shot Kirov as he walked down a hallway without his bodyguard, who died the next day on the way to the investigation in a suspicious accident of the NKVD vehicle, where he was the only one killed. When Nikolaev was asked why he shot Kirov, he pointed to the NKVD men and shouted that it was they who should be asked.

Kirov's assassination gave Stalin the pretext to liquidate his real or imagined enemies and competitors. He personally made a list of suspected conspirators in what he called the Leningrad and the Moscow Terrorist Centers, and in return for the promise to spare his life, Nikolaev "confessed" that he killed Kirov on orders from the Leningrad Terrorist Center. The trials of Nikolaev and the other suspects on Stalin's list were closed to the public, and they were all shot on the same night. Stalin ordered the NKVD to carry out death sentences immediately after they had been passed, and instructed the judicial organs not to permit any appeals that could delay the executions.

Two weeks after Kirov's assassination, two of Lenin's closest associates mentioned in his Testament, Zinoviev and Kamenev, were arrested together with five former members of the Central Committee and nine other party leaders. They were accused of forming an underground counterrevolutionary Moscow Center and charged with moral and political responsibility for the murder of Kirov. But Stalin did not wish to make his intentions too obvious, and for the time being they were sentenced to only five to ten years in prison.

It is difficult to imagine the effect of these arrests. All of a sudden, two great leaders of the Revolution and close associates of Lenin, whose portraits were everywhere and who were endlessly praised in the newspapers and at mass meetings turned out to be enemies of the people, and all those who had praised them became suspected of being their accomplices. To explain this turnaround to the population, mass meetings were held at factories, offices, and kolkhozes, at which members of the party competed with one another, loudly demanding severe punishment of the evildoers, and all who knew what was good for them shouted their approval and signed petitions demanding justice.

Subscribers to the *Soviet Encyclopedia,* which was sold only by subscription, were ordered by registered letter to cut out the pages with biographies that glorified Zinoviev and Kamenev and replace them with new pages. In school textbooks, the portraits and names of the new enemies of the people had to be completely covered with ink by the students.

At every meeting and in every speech, it was mandatory to praise Stalin as the giver of everything, and immediately upon hearing the holy name, the audience would jump to its feet and begin applauding. Knowing that NKVD spies were present at every meeting, no one wanted to be the first to stop, and they kept applauding and applauding, until after a long time the speaker had the courage to give a sign that it was safe to stop. In the press, the standard description of this performance was that the mention of the great Stalin's name evoked a stormy applause that turned into an ovation.

I heard the shattering news from a boy on the way home from school, and when I told my mother that Zinoviev and Kamenev were enemies of the people, she screamed at me as I had never heard her scream before: "Where have you heard this? Don't you ever say things like that again! Do you understand? Never!!!"

Using Kirov's assassination as an excuse, the Communist Party began a purge of its members. Every member had to appear before a party meeting to prove his working-class social origin and be quizzed about his management decisions. As a result of these interrogations, the NKVD handed down 267,000 sentences in 1935 and 274,000 in 1936.

By 1935 the collectivized peasants had accepted their fate, and as the second five-year plan progressed, food rationing was ended and Stalin announced: "Life has become better, comrades, life has become more joyous!" Immediately, the propaganda machine produced millions of placards and banners with the good news. The schools were plastered with them, and school children had to sing songs praising Comrade Stalin, such as:

> Comrades, let's sing a song about the Greatest Man on Earth,
>
> The Greatest and Wisest of Men, a song about Stalin!
>
> He led us into battle for happiness and good fortune,
>
> He lit bright spring stars above our cheerful dwellings;
>
> So comrades, let's sing a song about the Greatest of Geniuses,
>
> The Most Beloved and Dearest, a song about Comrade Stalin!

This was in the year in which a decree was issued that twelve-year-old children could be subject to the death penalty, which became handy for extracting false confessions from prisoners.

THE SHOW TRIALS

Since Trotsky had been considered second only to Lenin, Stalin had to get rid of him first, and made him out to be an arch villain who presumably had connived with both the right and the left deviationists in planning sabotage, assassinations, and selling out the country to Germany and Japan. Therefore, in 1927, Trotsky had been expelled from the Party and exiled to Kazakhstan. But Trotsky was too prominent to kill outright, and in 1929 Stalin had him deported to Turkey instead. From there Trotsky went to Norway, but when the Soviet Union then threatened to discontinue buying large quantities of herring from them, the Norwegians ordered him to get out.

After Norway, Trotsky attempted to go to the United States where he had followers among the American Communists. When at an immigration hearing he was asked about his participation in the murder of hundreds of thousands in Russia, his excuse was that this had happened during a civil war and a long time ago (it had actually been only about fifteen years). Finally, Trotsky and his wife wound up in Mexico, invited by the muralist Diego Rivera, in gratitude for which Trotsky seduced Diego's wife. Another Mexican muralist, the Communist David Alfaro Siqueiros, probably on Stalin's orders, organized on Trotsky an assassination attempt, but it failed.

In the Soviet Union, whenever a new group was accused of sabotage or any other action against the Bolsheviks, it was immediately attributed to Trotsky or his followers, and stormy mass meeting in factories and offices denounced the arch-enemy and demanded his death. Trotsky was killed in Mexico in 1940 by an NKVD assassin who had insinuated himself into Trotsky's fortified house by courting Trotsky's secretary. When the news of Trotsky's death was announced, school children in the Soviet Union danced in the street, singing that finally, the arch-villain was dead. Of course, neither the children nor the adults had any idea what Trotsky stood for; being caught reading or even possessing Trotsky's writings would have been signing one's death sentence.

With Trotsky out of the way, Stalin decided to get rid of both the left and the right deviationists by linking them to Trotsky and accusing them of being involved in Kirov's murder. Because some of them had been comrades of Lenin and members of the Politburo, he could not simply do away with them and decided to do it in several public trials, beginning in 1936.

On the very first day of the first Show Trial, the world was astonished to hear the accused confessing to a series of crimes they could not possibly have committed. Zinoviev, who with Stalin and Rykov, had ruled after Lenin's death, confessed that he had known about Kirov's murder. He and some of the other prisoners who appeared to be well-rehearsed, also mentioned names of several people who were not on trial: the right oppositionists Rykov, Bukharin, and Tomsky, the left oppositionists Radek and Piatakov, as well as some other former critics of Stalin. Just the fact that their names were mentioned meant that they would be next, and on the last day of the trial Tomsky, one of the seven members of the Politburo, shot himself. In his suicide note, he wrote:

> Don't believe Zinoviev's brazen slander . . .
> Now I end this letter after reading the court's
> resolution that I should be investigated. . . . I feel
> that I shan't be able to endure that, I am too tired
> for such shocks as being put in the same dock as
> fascists. . . . I ask forgiveness from the Party for
> my old mistakes.

One defendant alleged that in 1932 he had met Trotsky's son, Sedov, in Hotel Bristol in Copenhagen, where they had conspired to sabotage the Soviet industry and murder Soviet leaders. This was not possible, because Hotel Bristol had been demolished in 1917.

Stalin personally edited Zinoviev's verdict prepared by Lazar Kaganovich, and told him:

> You must cross out the final words: 'The
> sentence is final and cannot be appealed.' These
> words are superfluous and make a bad impression.
> We must not allow an appeal, but it is stupid to
> put that in the sentence.

NKVD chief Yagoda's second-in-command, Nikolai Yezhov, supervised the execution of all sixteen defendants and then extracted the bullets from their corpses and put them in envelopes marked with the victims' names. Two months later, in September 1936, Stalin accused Yagoda of not being diligent enough in exposing the Trotsky – Zinoviev conspiracy and replaced him with Yezhov. In March 1937, Yezhov charged Yagoda with being a German agent.

Yagoda was put in one of his prisons, where a former subordinate and now his jailer, asked him if he believed there was a God. His reply was: "I believed in Stalin and did everything Stalin wanted me to do, and I had violated

God's commandments thousands of times. Now, look where I am, and figure out for yourself whether there is a God."

The second Show Trial, from January 23 to January 30, 1937, was that of the Left Deviationists including two more of Lenin's associates: the head of the State Planning Committee Georgy Piatakov, and Karl Radek, who in 1917 had returned to Russia together with Lenin in the sealed German train. Instead of signing a prepared confession, Radek insisted on writing his own, which prosecutor Andrey Vyshinsky found inadequate, and during the rehearsal told Radek: "No good. Redo it, all of it. Try to admit that and that. . . . You are a journalist after all!"

All but four of the accused were shot. Radek was sentenced to prison but was killed there in 1939. Trying to save his wife, he had written her a letter saying: "I have admitted I was the member of a center, took part in terrorist activity. . . . I don't need to tell you that such admission could not have been extracted from me by violent means . . ."

There was a joke whispered in secret about three people in the Lubianka prison. The first one asked the second why he had been imprisoned, and he replied "Because I criticized Radek," to which the first man exclaimed, "But I am here because I praised Radek!" When they asked the third one, he shook his head and said: "I am Karl Radek!"

The third Show Trial was held in 1938, this time it was of the Right Deviationists, i.e., of people who had disagreed with Stalin on the speed of collectivization and on when to end the New Economic Policy. When the left deviationists Zinoviev and Kamenev had been shot, the old Bolshevik Nikolai Bukharin told the prosecutor Vyshinsky: "I am terribly glad the dogs have been shot." Now it was his turn.

After a whole year of preparation, the trial took place on March 12 and 13 and included Bukharin, Rykov, and eighteen others. Before Bukharin had been arrested, he had defended himself at the Central Committee by pointing out that he had been close to Lenin, who had called him "a most valuable and major theorist of the Party; he is also considered the favorite of the whole party." Stalin replied: "You must see it our way: Trotsky and his disciples Zinoviev and Kamenev used to work with Lenin and had come to terms with Hitler."

Bukharin had been a member of the Party Central Committee since the revolution and was also a member of the Politburo and the Chairman of the Comintern, the Communist International that controlled the Communist Parties all over the world. As early as 1913, he had helped Stalin write an article in Vienna, and having been so close with him, now wrote him 34 letters pleading for his life. In one of them, he told Stalin that he understood what Stalin was doing, saying that to help the Communist Cause, it was necessary for him to confess to terrorist acts that he did not commit.

At the trial, Bukharin confessed to being a "degenerate fascist" and having worked for "restoration of capitalism." He finished his last plea by saying:

> The monstrousness of my crime is immeasurable, especially in the new stage of struggle of the USSR (Union of Soviet Socialist Republics). May this trial be the last severe lesson, and may the great might of the USSR become clear to all.

Bukharin's last message to Stalin, found after Stalin's death in his desk drawer, read: "Koba (Stalin's revolutionary name), why do you need my life?" He was executed on March 15.

WHY WERE THE HARDENED REVOLUTIONARIES ADMITTING TO CRIMES WHICH THEY COULD NOT POSSIBLY HAVE COMMITTED?

Hearing the revolutionaries, many of whom had survived years of imprisonments in Tsarist jails confessing to fantastic crimes which they knew would lead to their death sentences, much of the foreign press did not believe these confessions and could only speculate about how they were obtained. But the future head of the NKVD, Lavrenty Beria, had said that any man given to him for three days would admit that he was the Prince of Wales. The technique was rather simple: first, interrogations throughout the night with severe beatings to convince the prisoners that there was no hope for them. Then threatening to have their wives or daughters raped before his eyes, or now that twelve-year-old children were subject to the death penalty, threatening to accuse them of aiding their father in anti-Soviet activity. Knowing that they were doomed and that the only way to save their family was to sign a prepared confession and to recite it in court, they did it. But their families were not always left alone.

Bukharin's wife, Anna, was arrested, and their several-months-old son was given to her mother. Soon after, Anna's mother was also arrested and the child was put in an orphanage. Later that year, Anna was brought to Moscow and held in the infamous Lubianka prison. In her memoir, *This I Cannot Forget*, she wrote that she did not know the fate of her husband and learned it only after remembering that a friend of her father, who had spent many years in prison, had shown her how inmates communicated by tapping on the walls of their cells.

The Russian alphabet has thirty-three letters, and all that was needed was to arrange them in a matrix of six columns and five rows with six letters in each row, except for the last one. First one tapped the number of the line then, after a pause, the number of the letter on that line. When she timidly tried it, it worked: the prisoner in the adjacent cell asked her if she had heard about the latest trial and then said, "The bastards murdered Bukharin." Anna, at first thought, worried that the message could be a trick by the NKVD, but because the word "murdered" was used rather than "executed", she realized that the message was from a fellow prisoner.

Anna was questioned by Yezhov's assistant Beria, whom she had met when she was fifteen and had visited Georgia with her father. Beria had a weakness for young girls and at the time had been very attentive to her. Now as she sat across from him, she noticed on his desk a thick folder with her name on it. He offered her fruit and sandwiches, but she refused them. Then he said, "I should tell you that you look more beautiful than when I saw you last." "That's odd," she replied. "In that case, ten more years in prison and you will be able to send me to Paris for a beauty contest." Beria smiled, and asked: "What have you been doing in camp, what work?" She replied, "I have been cleaning latrines."

Beria questioned her about her husband's associates, and she told him that while she knew some of them, they were not close. From his questions Anna deduced that the woman with whom she shared her cell had reported her every word. In closing, Beria shouted: "You blab too much. If you want to live, then shut up about Bukharin! If you don't shut up, here is what you'll get." He pointed his index finger at his temple. Anna was given an eight-year sentence and sent to a Siberian Gulag where she spent not eight, but twenty years.

On the eve of Bukharin's trial, he wrote Anna his final letter which she would not receive for fifty-four years, when it was found in the Kremlin Archive in 1992 and was unofficially delivered to her:

> I write to you with a definite purpose, which I emphasize three times over: no matter what you read, no matter what you hear, no matter how horrible these things may be, no matter of what I might say — endure everything courageously and calmly. Prepare the family. . . . Do not talk carelessly with anybody about anything. . . . I beg you to use all your strength and spirit to help yourself and the family endure this terrible phase . . . and keep a grip on yourself — be like a stone, a statue.

THE TIME OF YEZHOV

Nikolai Yezhov was a diligent NKVD apparatchik (bureaucrat), who knew how to take orders and carry them out quickly. Because he was short, he wore high heels and he was known as a good singer of soulful Russian songs. He had only two years of elementary education but was an avid book reader and Stalin trusted him and kept giving him important assignments. His name, which in Russian means "hedgehog," was soon on posters all over the country showing Yezhov with spiny hedgehog gloves squeezing the throat of a fat capitalist with bulging eyes and a dangling tongue.

As soon as Yezhov assumed his position, he began purging the NKVD of Yagoda's underlings, who knew too much. Now the old torturers were being tortured by new torturers, and the old executioners were being executed by new executioners. In my town in Ukraine, the NKVD chief was arrested together with his wife. Their two children, one a girl in my class and the other a toddler, were put in an orphanage.

As quoted in the *Black Book of Communism*, in July 1937, the Central Committee of the Party issued an order that:

> All kulaks and criminals must be immediately arrested . . . and after a trial before a troika, the most hostile are to be shot, and the less active but still hostile elements, deported (to the Far North or the Far East). . . . It is the Central Committee's wish that the composition of the troika is presented to it within five days, together with the numbers of those shot and deported.

In effect, the committee was ordering that within five days the victims had to be identified, arrested, tried, and shot, and the results reported. According to Yezhov's report, 259,450 people were arrested and 72,950 shot. To make sure that the new NKVD functionaries would not be accused of inadequate vigilance, as was Yagoda, they began competing with each other to see who could eliminate more potential enemies, and by December 15 an additional 22,500 people were executed.

In February 1938, after the top echelon of the government in Ukraine had been liquidated, Stalin sent his trusted associate Nikita Khrushchev to restore order, and in that year, Khrushchev had 106,000 people arrested and 54,000 shot. My 36-year-old father was among them, but it was not until 50 years later, when Gorbachev became president, that we found out what had happened to him. A letter from the KGB informed my relatives in the Soviet Union that Father had been accused of espionage and executed. The letter also stated that he was being posthumously rehabilitated, which was an admission that he had been innocent.

Altogether, in 1937 and 1938, out of a population of around 150 million, some 1.5 million were arrested and 682,000 shot. This "Great Terror" period during Yezhov's rule from September 1936 to November 1938, became known as *Yezhovshchina*, "The Time of Yezhov."

But it was not only the terror from above that was so frightening. Just as terrible was the terror from below: the system had unleashed an avalanche of denunciations. All it took for someone to be arrested was a letter to the NKVD saying that they had overheard their neighbor criticizing the government or telling a joke about the situation in the country, and a nasty neighbor, a superior on the job, a competitor for promotion, or even a spouse, would disappear. No proof was necessary — the NKVD had a way of obtaining confessions.

THE MADHOUSE

By 1937, with the Gulag camps full, the NKVD quotas began specifying how many were to be shot and how many sent to the Gulag to replace the dead. In the book *Khrushchev, the Man and His Era*, William Taubman wrote:

> Often, it seemed as if a kind of madness had overtaken everything and everyone, including

Stalin. 'Party organs were reduced to nothing,' according to Khrushchev, 'The leadership was paralyzed. No one could be appointed to a high post without the approval of the NKVD. . . . but even NKVD approval offered no guarantees. Sometimes someone would be approved, and several days later he would turn up behind bars. . . . But then it turned out that the person who denounced him had himself been denounced. All this created . . . a vicious circle by which the leadership in effect put itself on the road to self-extermination.'

The NKVD was obviously getting out of hand, and when Stalin again needed a scapegoat to take the blame for the terror, he told Yezhov that he had "broken too many dishes" and in November 1938 replaced him with his assistant, and Stalin's fellow Georgian, Lavrenty Beria. As in the previous change, within three months Beria had arrested ninety-seven of top Yezhov's appointees, most of whom were shot. Rumor had it that, to avoid torture, when some of them heard a knock on their office door, they shot themselves or jumped out of the window. Occasionally the knock they heard was actually on the door of the adjacent office.

In Yezhov's desk, Beria's men found envelopes with the names of the executed Politburo leaders, each containing a bullet that had killed them. Yezhov was arrested and taken to the secret prison that he had himself converted from a monastery, in which the chapel served as the execution chamber. Under torture, Yezhov admitted to conspiring to overthrow the government and to negligence in having purged too few enemies inside the NKVD — only 14,000. He pleaded: "Shoot me peacefully, without agonies.

Neither the court nor the Central Committee will believe I am innocent. . . . Please tell Stalin that I shall be dying with his name on my lips."

BRINGING THE ARMY UNDER CONTROL

With the political opposition being eliminated, the other force that could challenge Stalin's rule was the army, which could conceivably overthrow the government.

The purge of the army began at the top. In May 1937, Marshal Mikhail Tukhachevsky, who in 1920 at the age of 27 was put by Trotsky at the head of the Army, was demoted to a regional command far from Moscow and from his fellow officers. There he was arrested, and together with seven other top officers accused of plotting with the Germans to overthrow the Soviet regime. After they had been tried in secret, their arrest was announced on June 10. They were shot on June 11· and their execution was announced on June 12, so that there was no time for his army associates to do anything to save them. It was rumored that Tukhachevsky's written confession was covered with blood. His court-marshal was conducted by eight generals, five of whom were later shot. To explain to the people how some of the top military men turned out to be traitors, Stalin ordered the regional party authorities to organize mass meetings in factories, offices, and collective farms, demanding death sentences for all traitors. There is an excellent movie with English subtitles on a DVD titled *Burned by the Sun,* about the liquidation of a top military man.

Tukhachevsky's wife was also arrested and was seen in a straightjacket during her deportation. His twelve-year-old daughter was put in an orphanage and later was arrested and sent to the Gulag for five years as an "unreliable element."

When the war with Germany became a possibility in 1940 and there were not enough experienced generals in the Soviet Army, several Gulag survivors were freed and reinstated in the army under strict supervision by political commissars. One of the generals was Konstantin Rokossovsky, who in 1937 was accused of being a spy and was severely beaten for refusing to sign a false confession.

WHAT DID STALIN HAVE TO SAY?

In his *Report to the Eighteenth Congress of the Communist Party of the Soviet Union (Bolshevik) On the Work of the Central Committee,* Stalin wrote the following:

Certain foreign pressmen have been talking drivel to the effect that the purging of Soviet organizations of spies, assassins, and wreckers like Trotsky, Zinoviev, Kamenev, Yakir, Tukhachevsky, Rosengolts, Bukharin and other fiends has "shaken" the Soviet system and caused its 'demoralization.' All this cheap drivel deserves is laughter and scorn. How can the purging of Soviet organizations of noxious and hostile elements shake and demoralize the Soviet system? The Trotsky – Bukharin bunch, that handful of spies, assassins and wreckers, who kowtowed to the foreign world, who were possessed by a slavish instinct to grovel before every foreign bigwig and were ready to serve him as spies — that handful of individuals who did not understand that the humblest Soviet citizen, being free from the fetters of capital, stands head and shoulders above any high-placed foreign bigwig whose neck wears the yoke of capitalist slavery — of what use that miserable band of venal slaves, of what value can they be to the people, and whom can they 'demoralize'? In 1937 Tuchachevsky, Yakir, Uborevich, and other fiends were sentenced to be shot. After that, the elections to the Supreme Soviet of the U.S.S.R. were held. In these elections, 98.6 percent of the total vote was cast for the Soviet Government. At the beginning of 1938 Rosengolts, Rykov, Bukharin and other fiends were sentenced to be shot. After that, the elections to the Supreme Soviets of the Union Republics were held. In these elections, 99.4 percent of the total vote was cast for the Soviet Government. Where are the symptoms of 'demoralization,' we would like to know, and why was this 'demoralization' not reflected in the results of the elections?

Even if the election results cited by Stalin were true, there had been only a single candidate who was appointed by the Party. Also, the people knew that according to rumors, the paper ballots fell one on top of the other in such a way that the NKVD could tell who had voted against the government's candidate.

Through the 1930s, campaigns were conducted against the real or imaginary deviationists from the official party line in economics, history, and literature. About 2,000 members of the writer's union were expelled, which meant that they could not publish their works and if they did not immediately find a job, could be arrested as parasites. Some were executed, and many committed suicide. The aircraft designers Tupolev and Korolev, who later guided the Soviet space program, were arrested and made to work in prison laboratories.

In Belarus, eighty-seven of the 105 members of the Academy, the organization of scientists, were arrested as Polish spies.

THE SPANISH CIVIL WAR

On the international scene, the Soviet Union became deeply involved in the Spanish Civil War, which began in July of 1936 when General Francisco Franco rebelled against the leftist Republican government. To back the Spanish government, Stalin sent 2,044 military advisers and NKVD policemen, and Soviet soldiers manned their new airplanes and tanks that they were testing in combat.

An International Brigade of about 40,000 leftist volunteers was organized by the Comintern (Communist International) to fight against General Franco's Nationalist rebels. Its largest contingent of about 10,000 was French, that by the time the war ended in 1939 had lost around 3,000 dead; the Germans and Austrians numbered around 5,000, of whom 2,000 died. The American Lincoln Brigade had about 2,800 men, mostly Communist sympathizers, some of whom were followers of Trotsky and were in for a big surprise when the Soviet secret police got hold of them.

The Soviets carried their attack on the Trotskyists quite openly, and as an article in *Pravda* of November 17, 1936, stated: "So far as Catalonia (a province of Spain) is concerned, the clearing up of Trotskyists and Anarchists has begun, and it will be carried out with the same energy as in the USSR."

The Spanish Communists, controlled by the Soviets, set up illegal prisons called *cecas,* a Hispanicized name of the Soviet Cheka. One of its prisoners later wrote that in a nearby cemetery the cekists opened the graves with decomposing cadavers and kept in them the more difficult prisoners. Other prisoners were hung up by their feet or locked in tight boxes with just a tiny hole. The most dreaded was the "drawer," a tiny box in which the prisoner could only squat. To discourage escape, the prisoners were lined up every morning in fives, and if one was missing, the other four were shot.

Of the 2,800 members of the American Lincoln Brigade, at least 500 were liquidated for being 'undisciplined members,' or of having 'oppositional tendencies,' meaning they were followers of Trotsky rather than of Stalin.

CHAPTER 8
STALIN AND HITLER

With his competitors for power out of the way, Stalin became an absolute dictator, and wanted to restore to the Soviet Union all the lost territories of the old Russian Empire. These were the lands the Bolsheviks couldn't hold on to after World War I: the western part of Ukraine which became part of Poland, Estonia, Latvia, and Lithuania, which became independent countries, Moldova, which became part of Romania, and a small part of Finland.

The ideal way to reconquer these territories would be to do it without a war. Stalin particularly did not want a war on two fronts: with Germany and with Japan at the same time. Germany was getting closer to the Soviet Union by occupying Czechoslovakia and menacing Poland, and Japan, which now occupied part of China and was testing Soviet strength and resolve by encroaching into Soviet territory in Siberia.

In 1938, representatives of England, France, and Italy held the infamous conference with Hitler in Munich, where they agreed to Hitler's demand for the German-speaking part of Czechoslovakia. Stalin feared that if Britain and France signed a peace agreement with Germany, Hitler would be able to concentrate all his forces against the Soviet Union, and decided to send a hint to Hitler that the Soviets might be interested in making a deal with Germany.

Hitler, who was planning to give Poland an ultimatum demanding the port city of Danzig, took the hint. If Poland did not give in to his demands, he intended to attack it in August. But, if England and France came to the aid of Poland and attacked Germany from the West, he also did not want to be faced with a war with the Soviet Union in the East. Since it was already June, Hitler instructed his ambassador to the Soviet Union to begin negotiations with Stalin as soon as possible. On July 21, Hitler told his Foreign Minister, Ribbentrop, that he wanted an agreement within 14 days because he expected fierce Polish resistance and wanted to avoid possible difficulties caused by September rains.

Seeing that the Germans were anxious to make a deal, the Soviet Foreign Minister Molotov handed Ribbentrop a proposal that gave Stalin all the lands he wanted, and Hitler immediately accepted it.

An aide of Hitler's described his reaction when he received Stalin's demands: Hitler, he said, "Stared into space for a moment, flushed deeply, then banged on the table so that the glasses rattled and exclaimed in a voice breaking with excitement, 'I have them! I have them!'" In spite of the urgency and importance of the situation, Hitler insisted that his personal photographer, Heinrich Hoffman, accompany Ribbentrop to Moscow, and instructed him to get a good look at Stalin's earlobes to see whether they were "ingrown and Jewish, or separate and Aryan." He was relieved to learn that Stalin's earlobes were not ingrown.

The meeting with Stalin began within an hour of Ribbentrop's arrival in Moscow, and when the agreement was signed, Stalin proposed a toast to Hitler: "I know how much the German nation loves its Fuhrer" he said lifting his glass. "I should, therefore, like to drink to his health."

The Hitler – Stalin Pact created havoc among the American and European Communists, some of whom had supported Stalin because they thought he was anti-fascist, and some even left the Communist Party.

Hitler did not think that England and France would go to war over Poland. On the eve of the attack, he assembled fifty leading officers and told them:

> For us, it is easy to make decisions. We have nothing to lose, everything to gain. Our economic situation is such that we cannot hold out for more than a few years. . . . We have no other choice. We must act. . . . Our enemies have leaders who are below average. (He called them *das Gewuerm* – the worms.) No masters, no men of action. . . . We need not be afraid of a blockade. The East will supply us with grain, cattle, coal, lead, and zinc. . . . The destruction of Poland has priority, even if war breaks out in the West. . . . I shall give a propaganda reason for starting the war, whether it is plausible or not. The victor will not be asked whether he told the truth. When starting and waging a war it is not right that matters, but victory. Close your hearts to pity. Act brutally. Eighty million [German] people must obtain what is their right. Their existence must be made secure. The greatest harshness. . . . Any failures will be due solely to leaders having lost their nerve. The wholesale destruction of Poland is the objective. Speed is the chief thing. Pursuit until complete annihilation.

Hitler's propaganda reason for war on Poland was to dress a dozen prisoners in Polish uniforms, shoot them, and place the bodies to be photographed in a position as if they were attacking the German radio station in the border city of Gleivitz.

The attack on Poland began at 4:45 a.m. on September 1, 1939, when a German navy ship, on a presumably friendship visit to Danzig, unexpectedly opened fire on the Polish fort. At dawn, fifty-five German divisions and 1,500 warplanes went into action bombing Polish cities and strafing fleeing refugees on the roads. But much to Hitler's surprise, the Soviet Union did not attack Poland at the same time. Stalin waited until September 17, after the Japanese had signed a truce in the conflict on the border in Siberia, and only then attacked Poland. The Japanese wanted a peace treaty with the Soviet Union because their main interest was in Asia, and they wished to make sure that they would not be attacked by the Soviets from the North.

As a child, I watched with great fascination as the endless columns of tanks and trucks rumbled down the cobblestone road through our town in Ukraine. The radio and newspapers were full of stories of how the glorious Red Army was liberating our Ukrainian and Byelorussian brethren from the horrible exploitation and poverty they suffered under the capitalist Polish yoke.

In the occupied part of Poland, the Soviets set the value of the Polish money, the Zloty, to be equal to that of the Soviet Ruble, which in the Soviet Union was not worth much because there was nothing to buy. And, within a few days, the Soviet soldiers bought out everything available in the stores. They were ordered to tell the natives that they were being liberated, and after all the stores had been emptied, the Poles realised that yes, they had been liberated — from their clothing, butter, sugar, and meat.

Soviet soldiers were also ordered to deny that there were any shortages in the Soviet Union, and, according to rumors, when they were asked whether there were oranges there, the peasant boys (who had never seen an orange), replied that of course there were — the Soviet factories produced them on three shifts.

To generate good will, the soldiers passed out brown packages with chopped tobacco stems, which in the Soviet Union were rolled into cigarettes using bits of newspaper. The puzzled Poles, who had real tobacco, had no idea what to do with it. Regarding the newspapers, there was a joke that when someone in the Soviet Union was asked whether he was familiar with a particular newspaper, the usual reply was "No, I've never smoked it."

In school, we were told to ink out in our textbooks all negative references to German Fascists, and even the word "Fascist" was forbidden. The new politically correct designation was "National Socialists," and since we lived in the Union of Soviet Socialist Republics, to us, one socialist was as good as another.

In October 1939, immediately following the division of Poland between Germany and the Soviet Union, the Soviets demanded Estonia, Latvia, and Lithuania to permit Soviet troops to be stationed on their territory, to which they had no choice but to agree. The Soviet army occupied the three Baltic countries and in July 1940 the small local Communist parties organized meetings demanding that their country becomes part of the Soviet Union, to which after rigged elections, the Soviets generously agreed.

Soviet-style governments were set up in each country, and the NKVD rounded up businessmen, former officers, clergymen, and intellectuals. Those who were not shot were shipped together with their families to Siberia in cattle cars. In June 1940 came the turn of Moldova, which had been part of Romania. All these acquisitions had been agreed upon with Hitler in the special secret protocol.

As part of their agreement, the Soviet Union allowed Germany to use the ice-free Soviet port Murmansk to supply and repair their ships and U-boats that operated in the Northern Atlantic. The Soviets also supplied Germany one million tons of grain and 900,000 tons of petroleum. As Hitler had predicted, the Soviets allowed shipment of goods from Iran and the Far East through their territory, thereby breaking the British blockade of Germany.

In the Soviet-occupied part of Poland, the Soviet secret police arrested and executed thousands of "enemies of the people," including socialists and those Communists who were suspected of being followers of Trotsky rather than Stalin. They also murdered more than 20,000 Polish army officers who were their prisoners of war, whose mass graves were later discovered by the Germans in the Katyn Forest. The Soviets claimed that they had been killed by the Germans, but after the Soviet Union collapsed the President of Russia Yeltsin admitted it was the NKVD.

During the purges of 1937 – 1938, thousands of foreign Communist members of the Comintern were imprisoned and sent to the Gulag on suspicion of being followers of Trotsky, and in February 1940, the NKVD handed over 570 German Communists to the German secret police — the Gestapo. Among them was Margarete Buber-Neumann, who, when Hitler came to power in 1933, escaped together with her Communist husband to the Soviet Union. In 1937 he was arrested and shot, and she, as the wife of an enemy of the people, was sent to a Siberian Gulag. In her book *Prisoner of Hitler and Stalin,* she described her experiences in the Gulag and in a German concentration camp. She survived, and in 1949 testified at a trial in France when a Soviet defector, Victor Kravchenko, sued a French Communist newspaper that claimed his book *I Choose Freedom,* describing Soviet concentration camps, was not true. Kravchenko won the case.

*   *   *

Stalin was disappointed when in May 1940 the German Army in a few weeks defeated the superior French and British forces. He had hoped that both sides would exhaust themselves so that then the Soviet Army would be able to march across Europe without much resistance. This is why he had deployed the Soviet Army and Air Force in forward positions, far in front of the defensive line erected before the Hitler – Stalin Pact.

Hitler was aware of the disposition of Soviet forces, and on December 18, 1940, ordered his General Staff to prepare plans for attacking the Soviet Union on May 15, 1941. He called it Operation Barbarossa, after the medieval German emperor who had expanded Germany to the East. Hitler was not worried about the United States, whose army at that time was smaller than that of Greece or of Belgium.

After the lightning victory in France, Hitler was convinced that the German Army needed only two or three months to destroy the Soviet forces and conquer the European part of Russia before winter, and therefore was not concerned about winter uniforms for its soldiers or cold-weather lubricants for the Army's tanks and trucks.

In 1945, Hitler claimed that he had had no choice:

> I had no more difficult decision to take than the attack on Russia. I had always said we must avoid a two front war at all costs, and no one will doubt that I more than anyone reflected on Napoleon's Russian experience.

> Then why this war against Russia? And why at the time I chose? . . . Our only chance of defeating Russia lay in anticipating her. . . . Time was working against us. . . . In the course of the final weeks, I was obsessed with the fear that Stalin might forestall me.

Hitler saw Ukraine and European Russia as an indispensable granary for feeding the future German Empire and considered the Baku oil fields on the Caspian Sea indispensable for its industry and the military. For the rest of the Soviet Union, Hitler's economics department submitted a report stating:

> The population of the (more northerly) Russian regions, especially the urban, will have to look forward toward the severest famine. They will have to migrate to Siberia. . . . Efforts to save the population from starving to death by bringing surplus food from the black soil region can be made only at the expense of feeding Europe. They would undermine Germany's ability to hold out in the war and to withstand the blockade. . . . From this . . . there follows the extinction of industry as well as of large percentage of human beings in the hitherto deficit areas of Russia.

The attack on the Soviet Union was planned for May 15, 1941. But because Germany's Italian allies, without consulting Hitler, had attacked Greece but were driven back, he had to send a large force to help them, and the planned time of the attack had to be delayed by more than a month to June 22nd. It is possible that if Hitler could have kept his schedule and attacked on May 15, he could have achieved most of his objectives before the onset of winter, and the course of the war might have been quite different.

CHAPTER 9

WORLD WAR II: 1941 – 1945

The earliest warning of an imminent German attack on the Soviet Union came to Stalin in March 1941 from the U.S. Undersecretary of State Sumner Welles, who passed on information American agents had picked up in Berlin. Churchill sent another message in April. On March 3rd, the German-born journalist and Soviet spy Richard Sorge sent a report from Japan giving the date of attack as June 20th. According to the Soviet Marshal Zhukov's memoirs, Soviet intelligence reported to Stalin on March 20th that the date of the attack would be sometime from May 20th to mid-June. The spies also correctly identified the objectives of the three German groups and even the names of their commanders. But Stalin dismissed these reports as British disinformation intended to damage the Soviet – German relationship.

In the meantime, German planes continued to fly over the Soviet borders –one even flew all the way to Moscow, but Stalin prohibited firing upon them to avoid giving Hitler a pretext for an attack. He had personally given permission to German officers, who pretended to be looking for the remains of German soldiers from World War I, to explore the border area, and they had learned the location of Soviet telephone lines and the positions of their troops.

At 8 p.m. on June 21ˢᵗ, a German defector warned that the attack would be on the next morning, but Stalin said that it was another British attempt at misleading him and ordered the defector shot. He then issued his Directive #1 ordering Soviet forces not to fire and not to yield to any provocations, and the last Soviet supply train to Germany left during that night.

At 3:45 a.m. on June 22, Stalin was awakened and told that German planes were bombing cities in Ukraine, Belarus, Crimea, and the Baltics. He was asked for permission to return fire, but he again refused and insisted that this was only a provocation and that if the German generals needed a provocation, they would bomb even their own cities. He ordered Molotov to call the German ambassador, and Molotov was told that the ambassador had an important statement to make to His Excellency the People's Commissar of Foreign Affairs, Mr. Molotov. At 7:45 a.m. while Molotov was away, reports came that German armies were crossing the border, but Stalin said to wait for Molotov's return.

When Molotov came back all shaken and said that the German government had declared war on the Soviet Union, Stalin issued Directive #2, ordering his troops to destroy the enemy but, except for the air force, not to cross the border.

Because the German commandos knew the location of the telephone lines and had cut them, the Soviet High Command had no way to know what was happening on the front lines. While the German armies communicated by radio, the Soviets were still using telephones, because they thought that radio could be overheard.

In his memoir *On Military Service*, the Deputy Commissar of Defense, General Nikolay Voronov, recalls that "Stalin was depressed, nervous, and off balance. When he gave assignments, he demanded that they be completed in an unbelievably short time, without considering real possibilities."

According to the Soviet General Dmitri Volkogonov, Stalin believed that the German advance would be halted within a week, and had Molotov address the nation on the first day so that he would then be able to claim victory.

It was only after Stalin was shown the situation at Minsk, where two Panzer forces were encircling Soviet troops and nothing could be done to prevent it, that he appeared to have realized the situation. Volkogonov wrote:

> Stalin, usually so outwardly calm and deliberate in his speech and motions, could not restrain himself. He burst out with angry, insulting scolding. Then, without looking at anyone, head down and stooped over, he left the building, got into his car and went home.

Another report says that when Stalin shouted "Where are the commanders?" his old friend Marshal Voroshilov replied, "You had them all shot."

For several days Stalin was in a state of shock. In her book *Only One Year,* his daughter, Svetlana, wrote:

> He had not guessed or foreseen that the pact of 1939, which he had considered the outcome of his own great cunning, would be broken by an enemy more cunning than himself. This was the real reason for his deep depression at the start of the war. It was his immense political miscalculation.

While Stalin was in a state of shock at his dacha (summer home), no one dared make any major decisions, and on June 30, when Molotov and other members of the Politburo came to the dacha, he asked them why they came. The Commissar for Foreign Trade, Mikoyan, later wrote: "We found him in an armchair in the small dining room. He looked up and said, 'What have you come for?' He had the strangest look on his face, and the question itself was also rather strange. After all, he should have called us in." When Molotov suggested that a State Defense Committee should be set up with Stalin as the chairman, he looked surprised and agreed. Stalin returned to the Kremlin and in August took on the title of Supreme Commander.

Stalin's enigmatic behavior was clarified at a victory dinner on May 24, 1945, in which he remarked that "A different people would have said to the government 'You have failed to justify our expectations. Go away. We shall install another government which will conclude peace with Germany.'" It appears that he expected the visitors to dismiss him, which a majority in the Politburo had the power to do, and which was the reason why he had killed all the members of Lenin's Politburo.

Total confusion reigned in the Soviet armies: units could not communicate with each other or with the headquarters, many were surrounded and annihilated, others had received the Directive #3, an order to attack on all fronts, and not daring to disobey the order to attack, did so without coordination with other units only to be decimated. In order to escape encirclement by the German Panzers near Bialystok, the veteran of the Spanish Civil War, General Dmitri Pavlov, disobeyed the order to attack and pulled his troops back, but by June 29 lost contact with them. The next day, he was recalled to Moscow with his staff, where they were tortured until they confessed to having been part of a conspiracy against Stalin, and shot. Stalin himself approved the sentences but added: "but get rid of that rubbish about the conspiratorial activity. No appeal. Then inform the fronts." On September 5, Stalin signed an execution order for a list of 170 political prisoners, and four more generals were shot in October without a trial.

The Soviet army was larger than the German army. It had 4,826,900 men, 2,900,000 of whom were on the Western border. It also had 14,200 tanks against the German 3,350, and 9,200 aircraft against the German 2,000. But because of their short range, the Soviet aircraft were located along the western border, where 1,500 of them were destroyed on the ground.

The top commanders (with the rank of Marshal) were mostly old cavalrymen who had insisted that mechanization was unnecessary and that horse-drawn artillery was better than motorized because horses could be fed grass and did not need a supply of gasoline. They were opposed by the younger commanders like Zhukov and officers like Rokossovsky, who had recently been released from Gulag. The brightest commanders, like Tukhachevsky, who had studied German tactics and advocated mechanization, had been executed in 1938.

Finally, at 6:30 a.m. on July 3, eleven days after the German attack, Stalin in his heavy Georgian accent addressed the nation: "Comrades! Citizens! Brothers and sisters! Soldiers and sailors! I am addressing you, my friends!" He announced that the enemy's best divisions and aviation units had already been defeated, but the Motherland was still in serious danger and called for a guerilla war in the occupied areas and destruction of everything that could be useful to the enemy, including burning the grain fields. He did not say how people would survive without bread. He also did not say that this was a war for Communism — instead, he called it the Great Patriotic War.

In August, as the number of captured Soviet troops approached 3 million, Stalin issued Order #16, declaring that officers and commissars taken prisoner by the Germans would be regarded as "malicious deserters" and their families would be subject to arrest: "Everyone who has been captured is a traitor to the Motherland." This was the same hostage taking tactic used by Trotsky during the Civil War, and the reason that prisoners who had survived German captivity and returned home after the war, were sent to Siberia.

The German army was divided into three groups: Group North headed through the Baltic countries toward Leningrad and Group South aimed toward Kiev; Group Center, spearheaded by two Panzer divisions, had in the first ten days advanced 350 miles toward Moscow. In Ukraine, the German ally's Romanian army retook Moldova and headed toward Odessa.

By September 13, the Germans had surrounded Leningrad and on October 7, there was only a thin line of Soviet troops standing between the German army and Moscow. On October 10, Stalin put Zhukov in charge of defending Moscow, where only about 90,000 soldiers remained to defend the 150-mile front. Hitler's press chief announced to correspondents that "For all military purposes Soviet Russia is done with."

On October 15, Stalin ordered evacuation of the government from Moscow to Kuybyshev, 600 miles to the East. Offices and factories were abandoned, roads were jammed with fleeing party officials, stores were plundered, and prisoners were slaughtered in jails. Demolition squads mined bridges and railroads, and volunteer men and women were given arms. Stalin also considered leaving Moscow, but Zhukov reassured him that it could be held, and he remained. Also, having been assured by the spy Richard Sorge from Tokyo that the Japanese were not planning to attack the Soviet Union, about 750,000 well-equipped troops, together with 1,700 tanks and 1,500 aircraft were shifted from the Far East toward the Western Front.

By the middle of October, sleet and rain turned the mostly unpaved roads into rivers of mud, making it impossible for even tracked vehicles to advance, and the cloud cover impeded activities of the German Luftwaffe (air force). By the end of October, the German army had to halt for reinforcements, but they had for this only one railroad, while the Soviets had six rail supply lines bringing reinforcements from Siberia.

During this pause, Zhukov was able to reinforce the defenses less than fifty miles from Moscow with 100,000 men and 300 tanks. But the final battle for the city did not begin until November 15, after the weather had cleared and the tanks could travel easier on frozen ground. By the first week of December, the Germans had captured a terminus of the Moscow streetcar system and with binoculars could see the cupolas of the Kremlin churches. Then, on December 5, deep snow covered the ground, and the temperature fell to below 30 degrees F, with a bitter wind. The German forces did not have winter uniforms, and with their equipment frozen up, their advance came to a halt. At this point Zhukov threw in 750,000 fresh, well-equipped, and warmly dressed Siberian forces who were accustomed to cold weather. Many were even on skis. They counterattacked and threw the Germans back.

The German troops suffered 100,000 cases of frostbite. Their Panzer commander, General Hainz Guderian, later wrote: "Only he who saw the endless expanse of Russian snow during this winter of our misery and felt the icy wind that blew across it, can truly judge the events that now occurred."

For 1942, Hitler set an objective of obtaining needed oil from Baku, south of the Caucasian mountains, in the Soviet Republic of Azerbaijan. Capturing Baku would have deprived the Soviet army and industry of their major fuel supply, and Hitler split the Army Group South into two: one group heading to Baku, and the other, to protect the first one from being cut off, headed to the Volga River at Stalingrad. If this army had reached the Caspian Sea, it would have cut off the trans-Caucasian republics of Georgia, Armenia, and Azerbaijan from the rest of the Soviet Union.

While Soviet intelligence had managed to obtain the German operational orders to capture Stalingrad, the suspicious Stalin insisted that these orders were planted to deceive him and that the real German objective was to capture Moscow and Leningrad.

In 1942, Stalin hoped to push the Germans back from Moscow, lift the siege of Leningrad, recover the city of Kharkov in Ukraine, and liberate Crimea. Hitler's 1942 summer offensive was only half the size of the initial one in 1941. In September, Southern Group reached the Caucasian mountains, and its Mountaineer Unit planted the swastika flag on the peak of Mount Elbrus, the highest mountain in Europe. But when its advance stalled, the enraged Hitler fired the commanding general and appointed himself commander of this Group.

On August 23, 1942, the German Panzer division reached the Volga River in the northern suburb of Stalingrad, and on September 13, the Germans, with a force of 90,000 men,

2,000 canons, 300 tanks, and 1,000 aircraft controlling the skies, launched an all-out air and ground assault. They entered the city, but the Soviet army outnumbered two to one, fought them from street to street and building to building, sometimes in hand-to-hand combat, and often regained by night what it had lost during the day.

In his book *Life and Fate,* the war correspondent Vassily Grossman, who was there, quotes the Soviet Commanding General Vasily Chuikov:

> The many thousands of women and children left behind in the city sought shelter in the cellars of ruins, in sewers and caves. . . . They faced the virtual impossibility of finding food and water. Each time there was a lull in the bombardments, they appeared out of holes in the ground to cut slabs of meat off dead horses. . . . The chief foragers were children. . . . German soldiers made use of Stalingrad orphans. Daily tasks such as filling water bottles were dangerous when Russian snipers lay in wait for any movement. So, for the promise of a crust of bread, they would get Russian boys and girls to take their water bottles down to the Volga's edge to fill them. When the Soviet side realized what was happening, Red Army soldiers shot children on such missions. . . . That the Soviet regime was almost as unforgiving towards its own soldiers as towards the enemy is demonstrated by the total figure of 13,500 executions, both summary and judicial, during the battle of Stalingrad.

By October 14, all the Soviets had left was a bridgehead 4,000 yards from the Volga River, which was quickly reduced to only 1,000 yards, and after fifteen days and nights of constant fighting, both sides were exhausted. On November 11 the Germans attacked again. This time, the floating ice in the river made it impossible to resupply the defenders and they were running out of ammunition. But, they still managed to hold on to the bridgehead for one more week.

On November 19, after a heavy artillery barrage on a 200-mile wide front, a Soviet force of a million men hit and broke through north and south of Stalingrad. They hit the sectors held not by German units but by their allies the Romanians, whose fighting ability was considered inferior to that of the Germans. On November 21, the two Soviet Armies linked up and surrounded the German Sixth Army that consisted of twenty-two divisions.

The German General Friedrich von Paulus asked Hitler's permission to break out, but Hitler forbade any retreat and promised to supply 400 tons of ammunition, food, and fuel per day. However, nothing even close to that amount ever materialized. The improvised landing strips could not take heavy planes, and as the ring around the Germans shrank, even the smaller strips disappeared. The German troops froze and starved, and on January 8, 1943, General Rokossovsky, called for their surrender. But Hitler would not hear of any capitulation and demanded that the Paulus's troops fight to the death. However, when the temperature dropped to twenty below, some soldiers began waving white flags, and on January 31, 1943, General Paulus surrendered to General Rokossovsky.

German defeat at Stalingrad showed the world that their army was not unbeatable, but it was not the largest battle of World War II. That battle took place in July 1943 at the town of Kursk, where a Soviet salient threatened to break through between the German Group Center and

Group South. German High Command had planned a pincer movement that, if successful, would have encircled the Soviet forces and would have been the German revenge for Stalingrad. But Zhukov set up several concentric rings of minefields and artillery, through which after many attempts the Germans could not break through. Then the Soviet Army counterattacked and broke through the German lines.

It was the biggest tank battle of the war, with approximately 1,200 tanks engaged in a single battle. The Germans lost about 70,000 men and 3,000 tanks, and, while the Soviet losses were greater, they still had substantial reserves, which the Germans did not. After this defeat, the Germans were unable to launch a major offensive again, making the Kursk battle the pivotal point of the war.

After Kursk, the Soviet army, supported by the increased output of factories that had been evacuated in 1941 to Siberia, went on the offensive. The Soviets were now producing 2,000 tanks and 2,500 aircraft every month, which was much more than the German industry, heavily bombarded by American and British Air Forces, could manage. Also, $11 billion worth of American Lend-Lease supplies were arriving through Iran in the south and Murmansk in the north, bringing large quantities of tanks, aircraft, artillery, trucks (Studebakers), jeeps (Willises), ammunition, gasoline, boots and food rations.

Leningrad, where about a million people perished from starvation and bombardment, was freed after a 900-day siege, and in the south, the Germans barely managed to avoid entrapment on the Crimean Peninsula.

GERMAN ATROCITIES

With the advance of the Soviet army into Ukraine and Belarus, the German atrocities against the civilian population became evident. Unlike in Western Europe, where Jews were sent to concentration camps, in Ukraine and Belarus, Jewish men, women and children were shot in ditches in the forests. The German propaganda minister Joseph Goebbels wrote in his diary on March 27, 1942:

> Starting with Lublin (a city in Poland), the deportation of the Jews from Government-General (Polish territory) to the East had been set in motion. It is a pretty barbarous business — one would not wish to go into details — and there are not many Jews left. I should think one could assume that about 60% of them have been liquidated and about 40% taken for forced labor... One simply cannot be sentimental about these things.... The Fuehrer is the moving spirit of this radical solution both in word and deed.

The chief of the SS (elite forces) and Gestapo, Himmler, told the SS teams selected for "special duties":

> I have to expect of you superhuman acts of inhumanity. But it is the Fuehrer's will.... Most of you will know what it means when a hundred corpses are lying side by side, or five hundred or a thousand are lying there. To have stuck it out and to have remained decent, that is what has made us tough. This is a glorious page in our history that has never been and can never be written.... You must listen to what I have to say and let it go no further. All of us have asked ourselves: What about the women and children? I have decided

that this, too, requires a clear answer. I did not consider that I would be justified in getting rid of the men — in having them put to death — only to allow their children to grow up to avenge themselves on our sons and grandsons. We have to make up our minds, hard though it may be, that this race must be wiped off the face of the earth.

SOVIET ATROCITIES

In addition to suffering from the Germans, Stalin inflicted upon the Soviet people his own variety of persecutions. When the Germans occupied Northern Caucasus and Crimea, they had permitted the practice of religion and small business activity, which was welcomed by some of the local people. When the Soviets returned, they accused the whole population of having cooperated with the Germans, and as punishment banished every single person of the local ethnic groups, including members of the Communist Party, to Siberia and Kazakhstan. While the soldiers of these ethnic groups were fighting the Germans, 119,000 NKVD troops drove their families out of their homes with only the things they could carry. As quoted in the *Black Book of Communism*, one survivor wrote:

In the tightly shut wagons, people died like flies because of hunger and lack of oxygen, and no one gave us anything to drink. . . . When they did open the doors in the middle of the steppes in Kazakhstan, we were given military rations to eat and nothing to drink, and we were told to throw all the dead beside the railway line without burying them.

It is interesting to note, that while the inhumane Nazis realized and admitted that they were committing horrible crimes, such thought had never occurred to the Communists while they were wiping out whole villages during the civil war, starving to death millions during collectivization, working more millions to death in the Gulag, or banishing whole nations from their ancestral lands. To Lenin, like other political or religious fanatics, these were not crimes but sacrifices for the better future of mankind, and he was quoted as having said that "In the future, everything will be understood and everything will be forgiven."

D-DAY, THE YANKS ARE COMING

After the D-Day invasion, when the Allies landed in France on June 6, 1944, there was nothing to stop the advance of the Soviet Army, except politics. For all practical purposes, the landing in France was not only to finish off Germany but also to prevent the Soviet Union from occupying all of Europe.

As soon as the Soviet Army had crossed the Polish border, Stalin installed there a Polish government consisting of former Polish Comintern members who had survived the 1938 purges. On August 1, 1944, when the Soviet Army approached the Vistula River across from Warsaw, the Polish government in exile in London ordered its underground forces (consisting of about 150,000 untrained and inadequately armed civilians) to rise up against the Germans. They wanted the capital of Poland, Warsaw, to be liberated by the Poles themselves rather than by the Soviets. They expected the Red Army to cross the river into Warsaw to join them, but Stalin ordered his troops to stay put and let the Polish civilians fight the

Germans alone. To help the Poles, British supply planes would have needed to land for refueling in Soviet territory, but Stalin refused to allow that. When Churchill urged President Roosevelt to threaten to withhold arms and supplies to the Soviets unless they cooperated, Roosevelt refused.

The Vistula River is only several hundred yards wide, and for nine weeks Soviet troops watched German planes bombing Warsaw into rubble. The SS troops quelling the uprising drenched wounded insurgents in gasoline and burned them alive, chained women and children to tanks as shields against ambushes, and burned hospitals together with nurses and patients.

On October 2nd, the rebels capitulated. Some 225,000 civilians had been killed and around 500,000 deported to concentration camps. When in January of 1945 the Soviet army entered Warsaw (which before the war had been a city of one and a quarter million) there was not a single building standing intact. However, some people were still living in the basements of the ruins under the menacingly looming parts of walls and upper floors.

As the end of the war appeared imminent, Roosevelt, Churchill, and Stalin met in the Crimean city of Yalta to determine the post-war shape of Europe and to make sure that Germany would not be able to start another war in the foreseeable future. Roosevelt's goal was to talk Stalin into breaking his peace treaty with Japan and to attack it. Stalin responded with a straight face that in order to convince the Russian people to go to war with a country with which they had signed a peace treaty, he required to entice them with territorial enlargement, and Roosevelt agreed that Stalin should have the Japanese Kurile Islands. Another one of Roosevelt's goals was to assure Soviet participation in the creation of the United Nations. One of Roosevelt's aides at this meeting was Alger Hiss, who was later accused of having been a Soviet agent, which meant that Stalin knew all of Roosevelt's bargaining positions in advance.

Stalin's primary aim was not only to retain the pre-war borders he had acquired in his pact with Hitler, but also to extend his control over the governments of neighboring countries both in Europe and in Asia. His second aim was to secure large reparations from Germany — $10 billions, industrial machinery, rolling stock, and forced labor — to rebuild the Soviet Union. While he did not get an agreement on German forced labor, he used for this purpose the German prisoners of war instead, only about 15% of whom would return home.

Churchill's primary objective was to maintain England's "special relationship" with the United States and to keep the United States involved in Europe, particularly since Roosevelt's view was that U.S. forces should not remain there for more than two years. Churchill also wanted to restore the European balance of power by restoring France, and not allowing the creation of a power vacuum in Germany that could be filled by the Soviet Union.

The participants at Yalta agreed that Germany must surrender unconditionally; that no individual peace treaties would be entered into; that Germany would be divided into four zones; and that Berlin would be governed jointly.

In Poland, a joke about the Yalta meeting was going around that Roosevelt, Churchill, and Stalin went for a car ride. At one point the road was narrow, and a huge bull stood there glaring at them. Roosevelt, considering himself to be the most persuasive, politely addressed the bull first, and asked him to let them pass, but the bull ignored him. Then Churchill threatened the bull, with the same result.

Stalin smiled and said that it was his turn. He approached the bull and whispered something in his ear. The bull turned around, raised his tail and galloped away. "What did you say to him?" asked the astonished statesmen. "Very simple," said Stalin, "I just told him that if he did not move, I would have him put in a kolkhoz."

As German resistance crumbled, on April 23, 1945, Himmler approached the Swedish Count Folke Bernadotte to act as a middleman in arranging Germany's surrender to the Western Allies, so that they could advance rapidly to the east and they rather than the Soviets, would occupy most of Germany. The Allies refused.

On the morning of April 29, between 1 and 3 a.m., Hitler married his mistress Eva Braun. On the following day they both took cyanide, and to make sure that he was dead, one of Hitler's aides shot him in the head. Their charred bodies were found by Soviet troops and autopsies were performed on May 8 by Russian doctors, confirming their identity. For some reason, Stalin did not want it to be known that Hitler was dead, and on May 26 told the Americans that he thought Hitler may have escaped and was probably in Argentina. The Soviets kept the autopsy results secret until 1968.

President Roosevelt died on April 12th, and his Vice President Harry Truman became the new American president. In spite of having been vice president, he had not been close to Roosevelt and did not even know about the work on the atomic bomb. Only on August 6th, while on his way to the Potsdam conference with Stalin and Churchill, did Truman learn that the experimental bomb test had been successful, and authorized its use in Japan. When Truman told Stalin that the United States had an extremely powerful bomb, Stalin did not show any interest or surprise because he had known about it from his spies long before Truman did.

During the conference, Churchill was voted out of office and Clement Atlee took his place as Britain's Prime Minister. When the conference was not getting anywhere regarding joint governing of Germany, Stalin suggested that the Eastern Zone should be in the Soviet sphere and the Western Zones in the Western sphere. When Truman asked Stalin whether he meant to establish a line down Europe, "running from the Baltic to the Adriatic," Stalin said yes.

The Potsdam declaration, signed by Truman, Atlee, and Stalin on August 12, 1945, stated that the victors did not wish to "destroy or enslave" the German people but to help them "prepare for the eventual reconstruction of their life on a peaceful and democratic basis."

CHAPTER 10
STALIN'S RULE AFTER THE WAR

When the war ended, the exhausted people of the Soviet Union expected some relaxation of Stalin's totalitarian rule. During the war, the persecution of religion had diminished, and churches were even requested to collect money to equip a tank division, which was appropriately named after St. George the Victorious. But, while at the beginning of the war Stalin had addressed the people as "Brothers and Sisters," as soon as the war ended they again became just "Comrades." And they were reminded that they must work harder than ever to rebuild the country, and must remain vigilant against "enemies of the people." The victory was now ascribed not to the patriotic people, but to Stalin's genius.

A large part of the country lay devastated and 25 million people were without homes. An October 1945 report to the Central Committee of the Party stated: "The population is torn between despair in the face of the extremely difficult material situation and the hope that something is going to change." Also, the grain harvest in 1946 was poor, and the bread rations were less than a pound a day per person.

To make things worse, Stalin issued a decree confiscating the private plots of the collective farmers, and another one entitled "The Defense of Farm Property," as a result of which 53,000 farmers were sentenced for stealing grain. When these decrees still did not prevent the starving people from doing what was necessary to survive, a new decree called "Attack on State Kolkhoz Property" was announced, under which 380,000 people received sentences from 5 to 25 years.

In the famine of 1946 – 1947, about half a million people starved to death, and war widows had to beg in the streets and steal food to feed their children. To survive, the farmers had to find odd, unofficial jobs and did not regularly show up for work on the collective farms. Then another decree ordered the deportation to Siberia "of all individuals refusing to comply with the minimum number of work-days in the kolkhozes and living as parasites."

After World War II ended, the new "enemies of the people" became the returning war prisoners who had been declared traitors for having surrendered rather than fighting to their death. Even those soldiers who managed to escape from encirclement and had either joined the partisans behind the German lines or made their way back, were suspected to have been captured by the Germans and recruited as spies. Also, the civilians who had been forcibly taken to Germany as slave laborers, were suspected of having collaboratored with Germany. To deal with the millions of suspects, in May 1945 Stalin directed military authorities to set up 100 processing camps, each capable of accommodating 10,000 returnees, for screening by the NKVD.

Of the 5.7 million Soviet prisoners of war, about 4 million had died in German captivity. Many of those who had been liberated in Western Europe by the Allies did not want to return to the Soviet Union but were forcibly sent back by the British and American authorities. Some were told that they were being transferred to another camp but when the train doors were locked, they were taken to the Soviet Zone, and there were many cases of individual and mass suicides. Among the returned, some were shot and others received long sentences in the Gulag. At the meeting at Yalta, Roosevelt and Churchill had agreed to Stalin's request for mutual repatriation of prisoners of war, assuming that as in the West, they would be welcomed. It did not occur to them that they would be sending them to a Siberian Gulag or worse.

In the areas that had come into Soviet possession by the Hitler – Stalin Pact of 1949, the Soviets were not regarded as liberators and were particularly cruel to the local people. In 1948, about 50,000 people were deported to Siberia from Lithuania alone, of which 21,259 were executed. A similar fate befell the Latvians, Estonians, and Moldovans, and around 300,000 people were deported from the formerly Polish part of Ukraine.

To restore discipline and convince the population that the Soviet system was the best in the world, all contact with the outside world was prohibited. A special permit was needed even to visit another Communist country. Not even a slightest criticism of the Communist system was tolerated. The popular satirist Mikhail Zoshchenko, who in one of his stories had described a man getting a better shave with an ax than with a Soviet-made razor, was expelled from the writers union, which meant that he could not publish and could be prosecuted as a non-working parasite.

STALIN'S FOREIGN POLICY

At the end of the war, all of Europe lay in ruins and was divided by what the British Prime Minister Churchill called "an Iron Curtain" into Soviet-controlled East and free West. In Greece, the Communists aided by the Soviet Union fought a Civil War against the democratic government that was supported by the United States.

To save Greece and reassure other countries, President Truman announced his doctrine of support for any country that resisted Communist takeover. He also proposed the Marshall Plan of rebuilding all of Europe, including Germany. The Soviet Union and the countries under its control were offered participation in the plan, but Stalin rejected the offer giving the excuse that it would infringe on the sovereignty of the participants.

To counteract the Marshall Plan, Stalin established the Comecon — the Council for Mutual Economic Assistance of Eastern European Countries, which made each country specialize in a different industry so that they would become dependent on one another and on the Soviet Union.

In the United Nations, the Soviet representative Andrey Vyshinsky, who had conducted the Show Trials in the 1930's, insisted that each of the fifteen Soviet Republics should be given a seat. The United States representative countered that in that case, each of the American 48 states should also be given a seat as well. Nevertheless, the Soviet Union did get three seats: one for the Soviet Union and one each for Ukraine and Belarus, both of which were part of the Soviet Union, but neither even had a foreign office.

Because Yugoslavia had not been occupied by the Soviet Army, its Communist leader Marshal Tito felt free to do whatever he wanted independently from Stalin, and threw out Soviet NKVD agents who were setting up a network in his country. According to Khrushchev, Stalin was incensed and said: "I will shake my little finger, and there will be no more Tito. He will fall." However, Tito was not intimidated, and his secret police rounded up and jailed Stalin's agents and supporters.

In occupied Germany, food was still being rationed three years after the war ended, and the stores were empty. This was partly because the American Assistant Treasury Secretary Harry Dexter White, later accused of being a Soviet agent, had given the Soviets the printing plates for the occupation currency that was being used in all four zones of Germany. The Soviets printed this money around the clock, and were using it to buy everything they could in West Germany. To put an end to this, the American, British, and French occupation authorities introduced in their zones of occupation a new currency, the Deutschmark.

The effect of the monetary reform was miraculous: store shelves that the evening before the announcement of the reform were empty, in the morning were overflowing with merchandise. The goods had existed all along, but instead of selling them for the worthless occupation currency, merchants sold them on the black market for American dollars.

In response, the Soviets also introduced a new currency in their zone and declared that it would be the only currency in all four sectors of Berlin. This was rejected by the Berlin City Assembly, which decided that in the American, British, and French sectors the currency would be the Deutschmark. In retaliation, on August of 1948, the Soviets blocked the rail and highway access to West Berlin, where about 2.5 million people lived, and for whom the available supplies of food and coal could last only about a month.

When the Western Allies were discussing the division of Germany during the Potsdam Conference immediately after the end of the war, someone raised the question of whether there should be a clause guaranteeing Allied access to Berlin, which was located deep in the Soviet Zone. But the consensus was that uninhibited access was implicit in the agreement and that raising this question would show a lack of trust in the Soviets, and the issue was never raised.

Now, the only way Berlin could be supplied was by air, and the Anglo-American airlift to Berlin began on August 26. Just in case the Soviets would think of stopping the airlift by force, three groups of B-29 bombers capable of delivering atomic bombs were transferred to Europe.

By the time the airlift ended in May 1949, it was delivering 8,000 tons of supplies a day. Seeing that the blockade was not working, the Soviet Minister of Foreign Affairs hinted that if a meeting of foreign ministers could be arranged, the blockade might be lifted. However, it became clear that to discourage Stalin from creating more problems, a permanent commitment by the United States to defend Western Europe was required, and on April 4, 1949, the United States, Great Britain, and France created the North Atlantic Treaty Organization called NATO.

In response, the Soviets launched a massive propaganda campaign against the West. Their propaganda technique was based on setting up front organizations that used names of well-known, non-Communist, anti-war groups but were controlled by Communists. In 1950, the Spanish artist Pablo Picasso designed the peace dove for the Stockholm Peace Appeal which had secured millions of signatures worldwide, including those of the whole North Korean army just before it attacked South Korea.

To eliminate drives for independence in the Soviet satellite countries in Eastern Europe, Stalin initiated a series of purges in which he used the same steps as in the Soviet Union: denunciation, arrest, torture, confession, sham Show Trial, and imprisonment or execution. The first of these trials was held in September 1949 in Hungary, where the interior minister Laszlo Raik was accused of being a spy for America and Yugoslavia. He duly confessed, and was shot together with two associates. In Bulgaria, fearing the same fate, the Deputy Prime Minister Kostov jumped out of the police headquarters window but only broke his legs; he was tried for treason and hanged. In Albania, the Deputy Prime Minister Xoxe was tried and executed for being a follower of the Yugoslav dictator Tito.

In a big Show Trial in 1951 in Czechoslovakia, the Secretary General of the Communist Party, Rudolf Slansky, and other top leaders were tried for treason. Of the fourteen, eleven were hanged, and three received life sentences. In Poland and Romania, many top Communists received long prison sentences. It is estimated that in these purges some 500,000 had been arrested in Czechoslovakia, 300,000 in Poland and East Germany, and 200,000 in Hungary.

The Romanian Communist leader Anna Pauker and her Communist husband were in Moscow during the purges, and there were rumors that instead of getting a divorce, she had denounced him as a follower of Trotsky, and he disappeared.

At the end of the war in Europe, the Soviet Union violated its non-aggression pact with Japan and attacked the Japanese Army in China and Korea. The Soviets occupied North Korea and installed as the head of the government a Communist Korean who had escaped from the Japanese and became a captain in the Soviet Army. With the Japanese armaments captured by the Soviets and given to the Korean and Chinese Communists, he organized the Korean People's Army. He adopted the name Kim Il'sung which means "become the sun," and by the time of his death in 1994, he was referred to by the North Koreans as "The Great Leader" or "Eternal President." Nine hundred statues were erected in his honor, and by having his son succeed him, he established the first Communist Dynasty.

In a speech on January 12, 1950, the American Secretary of State Dean Acheson did not include South Korea into America's sphere of interest. Then Kim Il'sung, who wanted to take over South Korea, convinced Stalin that the Americans would not go to war for South Korea, and Stalin, who already had the A-bomb, gave his approval to attack it, which the North Koreans carried out on June 25.

When the United Nations Security Council debated the attack, Stalin did not want to be accused of initiating the war, and to avoid having to veto the condemnation of North Korea, instructed his delegation to boycott the meeting of the Council. This made it possible for the Security Council to pass a resolution condemning the attack, and the defense of South Korea was conducted in the name of the United Nations. Troops from twenty-one countries took part in expelling the North Koreans, who had initially succeeded in overrunning almost all of South Korea.

Then, the UN forces under General MacArthur landed in the middle of the peninsula, cut off the North Koreans, and pushed their army all the way to the Yalu River on the border with China. The Chinese, who were assured by the

Soviet spies that the United States would not use nuclear weapons, crossed the Yalu River and pushed the UN forces back to the pre-war border along the 38th parallel. Truce negotiations began in July 1951, but the armistice was not signed until July 1953, after Stalin's death.

The Soviet relations with China were full of twists and turns. The Chinese Communists, with the help of the Soviet Union and with the weapons given to them in 1945, had organized the Chinese Red Army which won the Civil War against the Chinese Republicans. They established a Soviet-style Communist government headed by the Chairman of the Chinese Communist Party Mao Tse-tung. But because the population of China was about five times greater than that of the Soviet Empire, a rivalry had developed as to which dictator should be considered the leader of World Communism, Stalin or Mao.

SOVIET ECONOMY AFTER WORLD WAR II

According to Khrushchev, in 1953 — eight years after the end of the war — the collectivized Soviet agriculture still had not recovered to its pre-war level. In the case of livestock, it did not even reach the pre-revolution level of 1916.

The main reason for low agricultural production, was Stalin's refusal to provide material incentives to the kolkhozes. He increased the amounts of grain they had to deliver to the state by 50 percent, so that the peasants had no incentive to work harder to produce more grain if it was going to be taken away. Stalin also raised their taxes, including those on the small private parcels the peasants still had around their homes. As he had put it to the Finance Minister: "all the peasant had to do to pay the new taxes was to sell one more chicken."

Another reason, was Stalin's belief that in his infinite wisdom he could judge scientific developments, and that genetics, a theory that inheritance is controlled by some invisible particles, was a capitalist pseudo-science. The theory favored by Stalin was the claim by an agronomist, Trofim Lysenko, that acquired characteristics can be inherited. Lysenko had written to Stalin that the scientists, because they adhered to "bourgeois genetics," prevented him from achieving exciting advances in agriculture. As a result, about 3,000 biologists who disagreed with Lysenko lost their jobs for not being politically correct. Some were shot, some served long sentences, and some — including the foremost Soviet geneticist, professor Vavilov — died in prison.

One of Lysenko's ideas was to plant long belts of trees, totaling about 3,500 miles, that would prevent erosion and moderate the climate. It was adopted as "Stalin's Plan for Transformation of Nature," and was to be implemented by the kolkhozes at their own expense. It was actually started, but many of the seedlings had died before they managed to transform the dry climate, and the idea was abandoned. Stalin ordered four more grandiose projects called the "Great Stalin Constructions," one of which — a canal between the rivers Volga and Don — was to be culminated by a giant statue of himself, for which thirty-three tons of copper had been appropriated. The canal was dug, but the statue was never erected.

At the celebration of Stalin's birthday on December 20, 1949, the Soviet Academy of Sciences held a special meeting to honor "the Greatest Genius of Mankind" and issued a large volume showing Stalin's presumable contributions to various branches of science.

Stalin's personality cult was well expressed by his own addition to the 1948 edition of his biography. To the paragraphs, "His military mastership was displayed both in defense and offense. His genius enabled him to divine the enemy's plans and defeat them" he modestly added, "Although he performed his task of the leader of the party and of the people with consummate skill and enjoyed the unreserved support of the entire Soviet people, Stalin never allowed his work to be marred by the slightest hint of vanity, conceit, or self-adulation."

STALIN'S TEST OF LOYALTY

To Stalin, the best way to test the loyalty of his subordinates was to imprison or execute their close relatives. Thus the brother of his faithful sycophant Lazar Kaganovich was executed during the purges, and the wife of Stalin's personal secretary Poskrebyshev was accused of espionage and shot. The wife of the aged figurehead president Mikhail Kalinin was sent to the Gulag after having been beaten unconscious by a female NKVD officer, and even Stalin's closest associate, the Minister of Foreign Affairs Molotov did not escape such a test. After his wife went to greet the Israeli Premier Golda Meir, she was imprisoned under the pretext of presumably having lost documents with state secrets, and Molotov was forced to divorce her. She had been close to Stalin's wife, and because she was the last person to speak to her, Stalin suspected that she might know the reason for his wife's suicide. She was not released until Stalin's death in 1953.

When the United Nations established the State of Israel in 1948, Stalin immediately granted it recognition with the idea that it would diminish British influence in the Middle East. When the Israeli Premier Golda Meir came to Moscow, she was greeted by thousands of Soviet Jews. This enthusiastic reception made Stalin suspect that some Jews might become more loyal to Israel than to the Soviet Union, and a campaign was begun against the possible "Zionist agents of American Imperialism." To Stalin's dismay, his daughter Svetlana fell in love with a Jewish filmmaker and he was quickly dispatched for ten years to the Gulag.

Jewish schools, theaters, and publications were closed. The director of the Moscow Jewish Theater, Solomon Mikhoels, was arrested while driving with another man, and, not wanting the arrest to become known, they were both tied up and run over by a truck. Stalin's daughter Svetlana reports having overheard her father suggesting that it should be announced Mikhoels died in a car accident, and he was buried with official honors. Number quotas were created for admission of Jewish students to universities, and a rumor went around that Stalin was planning to exile all Jews to Birobidzhan, an area in Eastern Siberia that in the 1930's had been designated as the Jewish Autonomous Province. Initially, about 40,000 Jews went to live there, but since then most had drifted back to their old towns.

WHO KILLED STALIN?

Stalin feared for his life. His food and drink were tasted to make sure they were not poisoned, and at night his residence was ringed by troops with dogs. He never flew, and when he traveled by train all other traffic had to be stopped, and KGB (a new name for the NKVD) troops were posted every 100 yards. Two or three similar trains started out at the same time, and only at the last minute did he decide which one he would take.

The people closest to him had to be ready to drop everything and come to his all-night dinners, where they had to listen to old stories and laugh as if they had never heard them. He liked getting everyone drunk and was testing the old Russian adage that what a sober person has on his mind, a drunken one has on his tongue.

Later, Khrushchev wrote in his memoir:

> For some reason, he found the humiliation of others amusing. I remember once Stalin made me dance the hopak. I had to squat down on my haunches, kick out my heels and try to keep a pleasant expression on my face. But I later told Mikoyan: 'When Stalin says dance, wise man dances.' The main thing was to occupy Stalin's time so he would not suffer from loneliness. He was depressed by loneliness, and he feared it.

When two of Stalin's daughter Svetlana's aunts were imprisoned, she asked her father why, and he replied:

> 'They talked a lot. They knew too much, and they talked too much. And it helped our enemies.' He saw enemies everywhere. It had reached the point of being pathological, of persecution mania; it was all a result of being lonely and desolate.

One of Svetlana's two aunts went mad in prison, but the other, who had survived, told her that she signed all the accusations: spying, contact with foreigners, even having poisoned her husband, just not to be tortured. She said that "at night, no one could sleep for the shrieks of agony in the cells. Victims screamed in an unearthly way, begging to be killed."

In October 1952, at the meeting of the Central Committee of the Party, Stalin, to everyone's shock and astonishment, asked the Committee to accept his resignation, citing his age and the "disloyalty of Molotov, Mikoyan, and several others, who had acted as agents of certain Western governments." Of course, no one dared to propose accepting his resignation, and the Central Committee begged him to remain. He obviously did not expect his resignation to be accepted, and upon agreeing to stay pulled out from his pocket a list of the people he recommended for a new, enlarged Politburo, henceforth to be called the Presidium. The list did not include Molotov and Mikoyan, and this immediately ignited a rumor of an impending purge of the still remaining old Bolsheviks.

According to Khrushchev, "The government virtually ceased to function. Everyone in the orchestra was playing on his own instrument any time he felt like it, and there was no direction from the conductor."

The suspicion that Stalin was planning another great purge was reinforced when Stalin accused Beria's assistant, Victor Abakumov, the head of the Ministry of National Security, of a nationalist conspiracy for having killed a Dr. Etinger, who died in custody. Presumably, the reason Abakumov killed Dr. Yakov Etinger was to ensure that "a criminal group of nationalist Jews, who had infiltrated the highest levels of the KGB, would not be unmasked."

The allegation of this plot was a slap at Beria, showing that Stalin did not trust him, and Beria knew all too well what had happened to his predecessors Yagoda and Yezhov. Therefore, Beria might have been telling the truth when upon his arrest after Stalin's death he supposedly told his accusers that it was he who had saved them from having been purged, implying that he had caused Stalin's death.

As Stalin's health continued to deteriorate, he turned against his personal physician, Dr. Vladimir Vinogradov, who, according to Svetlana, was the only doctor he had trusted. The immediate cause of this was a letter he had received from a young radiologist, Lydia Timashuk, who had first come to Stalin's attention in 1939 when she proposed a competition for finding means of prolonging his life, "so precious to the USSR and to mankind." She was recruited as an informer by the KGB and now claimed that by using the wrong kind of treatment, the doctors were trying to kill Stalin and other leaders. Khrushchev later claimed that Stalin had set her up himself because he then took over the "Doctor's Case."

After Dr. Vinogradov had examined Stalin on January 19, 1952, and advised him to stop working because of his severe atherosclerosis, Stalin asked Beria "to sort out Vinogradov." Lydia Timashuk was questioned, and was awarded the highest Soviet decoration: the Order of Lenin. After her testimony, Dr. Vinogradov and fourteen other Kremlin doctors were arrested, and Stalin ordered that Dr. Vinogradov should be put in chains and the other doctors beaten. He told the investigator: "If you do not obtain confessions from the doctors we will shorten you by a head."

When the confessions were produced, he distributed them to the members of the Politburo and told them: "You are blind like young kittens: what will happen without me? The country will perish because you do not know how to recognize enemies." The official "results" of the investigation and the names of the doctors were made public on January 13, 1953. Six of them were Jewish and were accused of working for American intelligence and of conspiring to kill Soviet leaders by improper treatment. An article in *Pravda* under the headline "Murderers in White

Gowns" linked them with the trials in Prague, where eleven "Jewish plotters" had been accused of using doctors to kill Communist leaders, and were hanged.

A letter to the Party newspaper *Pravda* condemning the doctors and demanding eradication of the "Jewish bourgeois nationalists, spies, and enemies of the Russian people" was prepared, and sixty prominent Jews, including Kaganovich, were told to sign it. They did.

On December 20, 1952, Stalin turned 73, and since he was a Georgian (many of whom lived to be a 100), it was feared that he could be terrorizing the country for another twenty-five years. However, fate had something else in store. On February 28, 1953, Stalin, Beria, Bulganin, Khrushchev, and Malenkov watched movies at the Kremlin and then had dinner at Stalin's dacha until six in the morning of March 1. Khrushchev wrote that:

> He (Stalin) was joking boisterously, jabbing me playfully in the stomach with his finger and calling me 'Nikita' with a Ukrainian accent (it would be Mykyta) as he always did when he was in a good mood. So after this particular session we all went home happy because nothing had gone wrong at dinner. Dinners at Stalin's did not always end on such a pleasant note.

The Minister of Defense Bulganin, had once told Khrushchev that after a dinner with Stalin one was never sure whether he would be going home or to prison.

The next day was Sunday, and, as on any other day, Khrushchev awaited Stalin's summons, but it did not come and he went to bed. Then Malenkov called telling Khrushchev: "Listen, the Cheka boys just called from Stalin's dacha. They think something has happened to him. We'd better get over there; I've already notified Beria and Bulganin. You'd better leave at once."

The duty officers told them that at eleven o'clock Stalin always called to ask for tea or something to eat, but that night he didn't. They sent in a maid, who found Stalin on the floor of his bedroom, and they put him on the sofa in the dining room. The delegation decided that, as Khrushchev put it, "it would not be suitable for us to make our presence known while Stalin was in such a non-presentable state," and they all went home. The fact that they did not call for Stalin's doctor aroused a suspicion that, fearing the threatening purge, they did it on purpose.

Later that night Malenkov called again, saying that he was told that there was something definitely wrong and that they should go back to the dacha. Now they also called Voroshilov, Kaganovich, and some doctors, who found that Stalin's right arm and left leg were paralyzed, and he could not speak. The six Presidium members took turns staying with Stalin, two at a time, because no one wanted to be with him without a witness. The doctors told them that after this, Stalin would not be able to work, and may not live long.

On their watch through the night, as Khrushchev and Bulganin were keeping an eye on the doctors, Khrushchev said: "You know what post [Beria] will take for himself? . . . He'll try to make himself Minister of State Security. No matter what happens, we can't let him do this . . . it will be the beginning of the end for us. He will take the post for the purpose of destroying us, and he will do it too if we let him."

CHAPTER 11

AFTER STALIN – KHRUSHCHEV

Stalin's death was announced on March 5, 1953, and for those who held privileged positions and those who had been brainwashed by the incessant propaganda, it was a great shock. To them, Stalin had been an infallible, omniscient, and omnipotent god-like father figure. His body lay in state for several days, and the crowd to view it flowed between two rows of military vehicles parked bumper to bumper. Therefore, when a stampede developed on May 9th, people had no way of escaping and several hundred were crushed to death. Even a dead Stalin still managed to kill.

After that, he was gutted, embalmed, and put on display next to the Lenin's mummy in the grim mausoleum on the Red Square, to be viewed by the curious and worshiped by the faithful.

It was not a good omen that it was the head of the NKVD, Beria, and not Malenkov, his superior, who gave the eulogy at Stalin's funeral. Nevertheless, to the country and the world, it appeared that the power had been transferred peacefully. Malenkov became the Prime Minister, Molotov remained the Minister of Foreign Affairs, Beria became the Minister of Internal Affairs (which included the NKVD and the police), and Khrushchev became the Secretary General of the Party.

Beria immediately sprang into action — he had Molotov's wife flown to Moscow from the Gulag, posthumously rehabilitated Kaganovich's brother and granted his widow a pension, and freed more than a million Gulag prisoners (mostly criminals, leaving the political prisoners in). He also proposed that the top posts in the fifteen Republics be held by natives rather than ethnic Russians, and that the East German Communists should talk to the West German Social Democrats about a possible unification of the country. In other words, he began to act as a sole ruler in both domestic and foreign affairs, bypassing the Party and the ministries. Also, as the chief of the NKVD, he had files on all of his colleagues, and if he were allowed to build up substantial support by appointing his own people to important positions, he would be able to get rid of anyone.

Therefore he had to go, and Khrushchev began plotting against him with the Prime Minister Malenkov, the Defense Minister Bulganin, and with Marshal Zhukov, who had never forgotten that in 1938 Beria had tortured and executed many of his fellow officers. The plotting took place in parks or in the street because they suspected that Beria had bugged their apartments.

WHO WAS KHRUSHCHEV?

Nikita Khrushchev was born into a peasant family and as a boy worked as a herdsman. When he was fourteen, the family moved to Donbass, the industrial part of Ukraine, where he became an apprentice in a factory. After the revolution, he was elected a member of the local Soviet and joined the Communist Party. In 1922, at the age of twenty-eight, he was sent to a technical school, where he became a Party Secretary and then the Party Secretary of the District.

There, he was noticed by Lazar Kaganovich, who brought him to Moscow. In 1933 he became Kaganovich's assistant, and in 1935 succeeded Kaganovich as Party Secretary for the Moscow Region. Later, he became a member of the Politburo and after Stalin died, the Secretary General of the Party, surpassing his mentor Kaganovich.

The coup against Beria is described by W. Taubman in his book *Khrushchev: The Man and His Era*. It took place on June 26, 1953, at the meeting of the Party Presidium. Only Khrushchev, Malenkov, and Bulganin knew what was about to happen. To avoid arousing Beria's suspicion, Bulganin brought to the meeting several trusted generals in his own limousine. They were put in an adjacent room and told to enter when they heard a bell ring twice.

When Beria asked what was on the agenda, he was told it was "Lavrenti Beria." Malenkov's notes describe the accusation: "Enemies have tried to put the MVD (the new name of the NKVD) above the Party and the Government. . . . Beria controls the Party and the Government. . . . Comrades are not sure who is eavesdropping on whom. . . . Next. . . . Who wants to discuss it?"

Beria was replying to the accusations when Malenkov rang the bell, and Marshal Zhukov came in with four officers, who pointed their guns at Beria. He was searched, and his pince-nez eyeglasses were taken away. To get him past the room with his bodyguards, they were served sandwiches, and while they ate, Beria was spirited away to an underground concrete bunker at an army base. Army officers occupied the Lubianka MVD headquarters, and the Minister of Defense Bulganin told them that Beria had been planning a coup. Tanks were dispatched to disarm the two divisions of Ministry of Internal Affairs troops stationed near Moscow.

Beria appealed to his former comrades, sending them a note that he had never done anything to harm them: "Dear comrades, they are going to get rid of me without trial or investigation, after five days of incarceration without a single interrogation. I beg you not to allow this, to interfere immediately, or it will be too late."

As the prosecutor, Khrushchev chose Roman Rudenko, who had been the Soviet Prosecutor at the Nurenberg trials of the Nazis, and who later, as Prosecutor General, reported that "from a judicial point of view, there was no basis for the mass arrests of the late thirties, let alone the executions."

On July 2, a Central Committee meeting began, and for six days several hundred witnesses testified about Beria's actions. Six associates of Beria were also indicted and were cooperating, hoping for leniency. They described how Beria had beaten prisoners, others accused him of ordering murders, even a plane crash. One of them said that Beria stalked his twelve-year-old daughter and when she accepted a ride in his limousine, drugged and raped her.

During the testimony, Beria was jumping up and down, and the judge, General Moskalenko, whom Beria had arrested in 1938, had the buttons cut off from his trousers. The indictment was 100 pages long, and on December 2 the death sentences were pronounced, and all the defendants were shot.

With Beria and the death threat gone, the friction between the former allies, Prime Minister Malenkov and Secretary General of the Party Khrushchev, came to the surface. Both realized that things could not go on as before, and with long lines for food and consumer goods, the question became who could better feed the people.

In August 1953, Malenkov announced that the Soviet Union had the hydrogen bomb, and that the new balance of power with the United States would permit greater investment in consumer goods. Khrushchev, on the other hand, insisted that the armed forces had to be strengthened, which meant more investment in heavy industry. But before tackling Malenkov, Khrushchev — just like Stalin before him — used his position of Secretary General of the Party to fill its Central Committee with people who would be loyal to him.

In January 1955, without naming names, Khrushchev attacked the "theoreticians" who believed that at a certain stage in the development of Socialism consumer industry should be put ahead of heavy industry. He accused these theoreticians of "Right Deviation" from the Party Line — of views differing from those of Lenin, that "in their day were preached by Rykov, Bukharin, and their kind."

Being associated with enemies executed by Stalin, Malenkov could not defend himself. Pleading lack of experience, he resigned his post as Prime Minister and in February became the Minister of Power Stations. But there were still other potential competitors for power, and Khrushchev's problem was how to discredit them.

His solution came on February 1956 like a thunderbolt from a clear sky. Before a stunned audience of the Congress, Khrushchev made his famous four-hours-long "secret" speech entitled "On the Cult of Personality and its Consequences," in which he confirmed everything that anti-Communists had been saying for years.

First, he accused the revered Stalin of having murdered Lenin's disciples, of having created a cult of personality, and of ruling without consulting the Politburo. Then, he linked his rivals with Stalin's crimes. The speech sent shockwaves not only throughout the Soviet Union but also through the entire world.

Among many other things, he said:

> After Stalin's death, the Party began explaining that it is impermissible to elevate one person, to transform him into a superman possessing supernatural characteristics akin to those of a god. Such a man supposedly knows everything, sees everything, thinks for everyone, can do anything, is infallible in his behavior. . . . Stalin originated the concept 'enemy of the people.' This term automatically rendered it unnecessary that the ideological error of a man is proven, [and it] made possible most cruel repression. . . . The only proof of guilt was the "confession" gained with the help of cruel and inhuman tortures.

> The vicious practice was condoned of having the NKVD prepare lists of persons whose sentences were prepared in advance. Yezhov would send these lists to Stalin personally for his approval of the proposed punishment. . . . He approved these lists.

The shocked delegates could not believe their ears. If only a day before anyone had dared to say something like this, he would have lost more than his job. As some of the attendees recalled, the speech was met with deadly silence — some felt anxious and joyous at the same time. One remembers taking five nitroglycerin pills, while another wrote: "We did not look each other in the eyes . . . whether from shame or from shock or from the simple unexpectedness of it."

Rumors about the speech began flying within hours, and within days the speech was read at closed party meetings throughout the country, but nothing was published in the press. By June, Molotov and Kaganovich were out, and Stalin's body had been removed from Lenin's Mausoleum and buried near the Kremlin wall next to other Communist leaders.

Khrushchev was very careful to emphasize that the villain was only Stalin and not the Communist system, and while Lenin had always been the venerated father figure next to Marx, he was now endowed with all the admirable virtues previously ascribed to Stalin: infinite wisdom and knowledge, as well as kindness and concern for humanity.

Actually, as described by the *Washington Post* correspondent in Moscow, David Remnick, in his book *Lenin's Tomb*, a friend of his had met the former Foreign Minister Molotov and said that it was a pity that Lenin had died so early because while Stalin was a bloodsucker, Lenin was a noble person. To which with a wry smile Molotov replied that "compared to Lenin, Stalin was a mere lamb."

Abroad, the shock of the speech was not any less severe. The American writer Howard Fast, a recipient of the Stalin Peace Prize (Stalin's response to the Nobel Peace Prize), wrote in his book *The Naked God:* "With the appearance of this 'secret' report, the edifice that I had become a part of thirteen years earlier, came crumbling down in ashes — ashes of grief, horror, and hopelessness. . . . I may have been a fool not to know of this terror before." And even the leftist writer Susan Sontag wrote that the readers of *The Reader's Digest,* a conservative magazine, were better informed about what was going on in the Soviet Union than the readers of the general press.

In the countries of Eastern Europe, the reaction was explosive. Within a few days, Polish President Boleslav Bierut, who had sent many people to their death, dropped dead of a heart attack. On June 4, 1956, the US State Department published the text of the speech, and on June 28 a revolt broke out at the International Trade Fair in the Polish city of Poznan, and it took the Polish Army to suppress it.

On October 23, 1956, when the Hungarian secret police opened fire on demonstrating students, a revolution broke out in Hungary. Prisoners were freed and armed, and security policemen were attacked and lynched. A democratic government was established within days, and declared its desire to become neutral and to quit the Warsaw Pact.

On November 3, the Soviets invited a Hungarian delegation to discuss the situation. Upon their arrival, the delegates were arrested and later executed. The next day, Soviet tanks entered Budapest and suppressed the revolution. Some 2,500 Hungarians and 700 Soviets were killed in the fighting.

Concerned where de-Stalinisation might lead, the Soviet Press began publishing articles on its limits. Khrushchev's position was weakened, while the influence of Kaganovich and Molotov rose, and they felt strong enough to conspire against him. They could count on a majority in the Presidium (the new name for the Politburo) — the governing body of the Party — and wanted to enforce a vote to remove Khrushchev from his position as the Secretary General. However, Khrushchev insisted that such an important decision should be undertaken not by the Presidium but by the 300-member Central Committee, which he had packed with his followers.

Khrushchev called a meeting of the Committee and got Marshal Zhukov to send military aircraft all over the country to bring the committee members to Moscow. The meeting began on June 22. It lasted a week and turned into an unimaginable farce. It was like a fall-out of a band of criminals, accusing one another of having murdered thousands of people, with each proclaiming his innocence and pointing his finger at smeone else.

In *Khrushchev: The Man and His Era*, historian William Taubman describes the bedlam and quotes the participants. Marshal Zhukov began by accusing Molotov, Malenkov, and Kaganovich the "main culprits in the arrest and execution of party and state cadres." As an example Zhukov gave the execution of General Yakir, a friend of Khrushchev who begged Stalin for mercy. On the appeal, Stalin scrawled: "Scoundrel and prostitute," to which Molotov added: "A perfect description. Blackguard, bastard, prick," and Kaganovich wrote: "Only one punishment for him: death!" He said that between February 27 and November 12, 1938, Stalin, Molotov, and Kaganovich had personally authorized 38,679 executions. On one day alone, November 12, 1938, Stalin and Molotov dispatched 3,167 people "like cattle to slaughter," and the wives of the "enemies of the people also got a bullet in their head."

In his defense, Kaganovich insisted: "The whole Politburo signed the death warrants and provincial party chiefs, one of whom was Khrushchev."

Kaganovich to Khrushchev: "Did not you sign death warrants in Ukraine?"

Khrushchev: "We all gave our approval. I voted against Yakir and slandered him, many times, as a traitor. I believed the charges against him. . . . I assume you, Kaganovich, had checked into those charges, you were a member of the Politburo back then, you should have known."

Khrushchev's accusation was that Malenkov, Molotov, and Kaganovich, had hatched an "anti-party" conspiracy for the purpose of weakening the party by splitting it into factions. Molotov replied that there was no anti-party conspiracy, and it was just an accumulation of grievances against Khrushchev's arrogance: "He keeps calling for modesty, he lacks it himself. When we chose him as First Secretary, I thought he'd remain the same person he'd been before that, but it has not turned out that way, and it gets worse all the time." Then Zhukov reminded Molotov of his complicity in Stalin's crimes.

Molotov: "I accept that responsibility as do other members of the Politburo."

Khrushchev: "Who authorized torture to produce false confessions?"

Molotov: "All Politburo members."

Khrushchev: "Your hands are covered with blood, Molotov, your conscience isn't clean; you are a vile person."

The finger pointing went on for six days. In the end, Molotov and Kaganovich admitted their responsibility, but qualified it as only "political," to which Zhukov added: "And criminal."

Khrushchev said that in 1937 - 1938 one and a half million people were arrested, of whom 681,692 were shot. According to Molotov, it was Khrushchev himself, who as a member of the Ukrainian troika, had 106,119 people arrested and 54,000 executed.

On July 4, the Communist Party newspaper *Pravda* announced that Molotov, Malenkov, and Kaganovich had been removed from their posts and expelled from the Central Committee. Two days later, Kaganovich called his former protégé Khrushchev to plead for his life: "I beg you not to allow them to deal with me as they dealt with people under Stalin." To which Khrushchev replied that he would think about it.

In the end, Kaganovich was sent to manage a chemical plant in the provinces, Malenkov was sent to manage a power plant in Kazakhstan, and Molotov became ambassador to Outer Mongolia.

In 1957, Defense Minister Marshal Zhukov, who only a year before had saved Khrushchev's hide, was accused by Khrushchev of "Bonapartism" — acting like Napoleon Bonaparte, who had taken over power after the French Revolution. Khrushchev demoted him to Commander of the military district of Odessa, just as Stalin had done right after the war.

THE SAUSAGE COMMUNISM

Now that Khrushchev was the Secretary General of the Party and the Prime Minister, it was he who was quoted in every speech. At the same time he was claiming to be against Stalin's cult of personality, he was building one around himself, and just a mention of his name received a "stormy ovation." His film biography was shown on television and in the movies throughout the country.

To boost his popularity, Khrushchev now talked about consumer goods and food for the people, which were the same views for which he had banned Malenkov. At an agricultural convention, he said:

> We must produce more grain. The more grain there is, the more meat, lard and fruit there will be. . . . And, if there is sausage and fruit, then people will say: give us grapes, and with grapes,

one must have wine and all sort of other things. And these are legitimate demands.

He was also quoted as saying "What kind of Communism is this if there is no sausage?"

Khrushchev promised that by 1970 the Soviet agriculture and industry would be producing even more than the American, both per capita and in total. He restored the dominance of the Party, and now the Party Committees in factories, shops, and offices, would be monitoring fulfillment of the five-year plans. Also, he split the Party in two, one part supervising industry and the other agriculture.

The launching of Sputnik by the Soviet Union on October 10, 1957, and landing the first rocket on the moon on September 14, 1959 (a day before he flew to Washington in a giant TU 114 airliner), gave Khrushchev a great deal of self-confidence in dealing with President Eisenhower. He came to the conclusion that coexistence with the United States was possible, and that the Soviet Union would win the competition with capitalist countries. He cheerfully toured the United States and visited several farms, where he asked many questions about farming and the extensive use of fertilizers. He was particularly impressed by the septic tank systems in farmhouses and was disappointed that because of security considerations he was not taken to Disneyland.

But Soviet relations with the United States soured when in 1960, just before the summit meeting in Paris, they shot down an American U-2 spy plane. Later that year, Khrushchev came to New York to attend the UN meeting on decolonization and arms limitation, which he needed in order to be able to invest in agriculture. By coming uninvited, he also wanted to embarrass President

Eisenhower. In return, his delegation was forbidden to leave Manhattan. Khrushchev, just like Marx, Lenin, and Stalin before him, believed that all working people in the world were Communist sympathizers, but when his ship entered the East River he was met by longshoremen with placards: "Roses are red, violets are blue, Stalin dropped dead, how about you?"

Appearing on the second-story balcony of the Soviet delegation on Park Avenue and 86th Street, Khrushchev raised his clenched fist in a "Red Front" salute and sang the "Internationale," calling on workers of the world to rise up against capitalism. At the UN, when he did not like someone's speech, he banged on the desk with his fist and even interrupted a speech by the British Prime Minister Harold Macmillan.

When in response to Khrushchev's call for decolonization, a Philippine delegate said that the Eastern European countries were swallowed by the Soviet Union and are deprived of political and human rights, Khrushchev banged on the desk with both fists, then took off his shoe, shook it threateningly at the speaker, and began pounding the desk with it. The Soviet Foreign Minister Andrei Gromyko who sat next to him, looked embarrassed, but he also took off his shoe and tapped it on the desk. Khrushchev proposed that the UN headquarters be relocated to Europe and that the UN should be run by a troika of one Soviet, one Western, and one neutral representative.

In June 1961, at the summit meeting in Vienna, Khrushchev met President Kennedy, who was totally unprepared for a meeting with a wily peasant-type with a lot of street-smarts. Kennedy was sure he could charm Khrushchev the way he charmed everyone else, but Khrushchev did not appreciate Kennedy's charm and angrily lectured him on the inevitability of Communist victories all over the world, to which Kennedy could not give an answer.

Khrushchev told Kennedy that the stumbling block to peaceful coexistence was the refusal of the West to recognize the Soviet Union's right to assist the anti-colonial wars of liberation throughout the world. He also informed Kennedy that the Soviet Union would sign a separate peace treaty with East Germany, which would give it the right to deny Western powers access to Berlin.

In his book, *President Kennedy*, Richard Reeves quotes James Reston of *The New York Times*, who interviewed Kennedy at the American embassy right after his meeting with Krushchev. He asked Kennedy:

> "How was it?" "Worst thing in my life. He savaged me," replied Kennedy. "I think I know why he treated me like this. He thinks because of the Bay of Pigs that I am inexperienced. Probably thinks I am stupid. Maybe more important, he thinks that I have no guts.". . . "We have to see what we can do to restore a feeling in Moscow that we will defend our national interest. I will have to increase the defense budget. And we have to confront them. The only place we can do that is Vietnam."

Seeing that Kennedy had increased military spending and was actively promoting civil defense, Khrushchev, instead of signing a peace treaty with East Germany, on August 13, 1961, began building a wall around the American, British and French sectors of Berlin, in the hope that it would prevent the East Germans from escaping to West Germany.

About a year later, on August 22, 1962, the CIA reported to Kennedy that twenty Soviet ships may have arrived in Cuba with military cargo. Because the Soviet Union did not have many long-range or submarine-launched missiles, the only way Khrushchev could counteract the threat by American intercontinental missiles was to place his medium-range missiles within striking distance of the United States, which would also balance the American medium-range missiles that had been installed in Turkey. The only place where he could accomplish this was Cuba, which the Soviet Union had been subsidizing for many years by helping the Cuban economy and supplying them with oil in exchange for sugar.

With more Soviet ships heading for Cuba, the CIA estimated that the missiles would be installed sometime between December 1 and 15, and on October 18, Kennedy requested a meeting with the Soviet Foreign Minister Gromyko who assured Kennedy that there were no offensive weapons in Cuba. In his memoir published in 1989, Gromyko described their meeting as follows:

> On October 18, 1962, on the instruction of the Soviet leadership, I met President Kennedy in the White House.... Contrary to later assertions made in the West, at no time in our conversation did Kennedy raise the question of the presence of Soviet rockets in Cuba; consequently, there was no need for me to say whether there were any there or not. Furthermore, I told the president: 'Soviet aid to Cuba is aimed exclusively at strengthening her defensive capability and developing her peaceful economy. Using Soviet instructors to teach the Cubans how to handle defensive weapons cannot be seen as a threat to anyone.'

The CIA had estimated the number of Soviet "teachers" to be between 8,000 and 40,000, and in 1989 the Soviets admitted that there were 42,000.

On October 22, 1962, the State Department gave Soviet Ambassador Anatoly Dobrynin a warning letter to Khrushchev, and that evening President Kennedy addressed the nation which, until then, was not aware of the growing threat. He announced that he was ordering a naval blockade of Cuba, that if the installation of missiles continued there would be further action. And that if any nuclear missiles were launched from Cuba on any nation in the Western Hemisphere, it would be considered an attack by the Soviet Union on the United States.

The date to attack Cuba was set for October 30 when 90,000 U.S. Marines and airborne troops would land there. All armed services were put on alert, and sixty B-52 bombers were airborne at all times armed with 196 hydrogen bombs; their pilots carried sealed letters specifying their targets. Six hundred and twenty-eight other bombers with 2,026 nuclear bombs were dispersed throughout the world.

On the following day, a letter from Khrushchev was delivered to Kennedy just before lunchtime, accusing the United States of illegal aggressive act. During that day, the OAS (Organization of American States) endorsed the American action, which came as a surprise to Khrushchev, who expected Latin American countries to support Cuba against the Yankees. In his reply to Khrushchev, Kennedy expressed hope that Soviet ships would observe the terms of the quarantine of Cuba established by the OAS.

On October 24th, the Soviet ships halted, but at 2 a.m. a four-page letter came from Khrushchev saying the United States had no right to impose a blockade, that it was against the international law and the Soviet government would take measures to protect its rights, but the Soviet ships still turned around.

Now the problem was how to make the Soviets remove the missiles that were already in Cuba. On October 26, a man from the Soviet embassy who was listed as a counselor but was suspected to be the KGB Station Chief called the State Department with the suggestion that the Soviets would remove the missiles if the United States pledged not to invade Cuba. On the next day, another long letter arrived from Khrushchev, saying: "Dear Mr. President: I have received your letter of October 25. From your letter, I got the feeling that you have some understanding of the situation which has developed and some sense of responsibility. I value this." He offered a solution identical to that of the KGB caller. But several hours later, another letter arrived, demanding that the United States remove its medium-range missiles based in Turkey, in return for which the Soviet Union would pledge not to attack Turkey.

In the meantime, the clock was ticking, and the military was getting ready to attack Cuba in three days. Also, on the 27th came the news that an American U-2 reconnaissance plane had been shot down over Cuba. Kennedy had a standing order to destroy the missile site that fired on U.S. planes but decided to wait until the next day for an answer to his letter. If there was no answer, the U.S. would declare that its plane had been fired upon and would attack the anti-aircraft site. Kennedy asked his brother, Bobby, to tell Dobrynin that the response to Khrushchev's letter would be sent later in the evening, agreeing to the proposal that the missiles would be removed in exchange for a commitment not to invade Cuba and that the U.S. would remove its missiles from Turkey, but on a later date. He also asked Bobby to impress upon Dobrynin that an immediate reply was needed because the President could not resist the pressure from the military much longer. The reply came the next day via Radio Moscow, declaring victory and agreeing to dismantle and remove the missiles from Cuba.

It was a close call to a nuclear war, but the world did not find out how close until after the collapse of the Soviet Union twenty-seven years later. It then became known that the Soviet forces in Cuba were armed with tactical nuclear weapons and that in the case of an American invasion the Soviet commanding general had been authorized to use them at his discretion.

To punish Cuba, Kennedy ordered an embargo on exports of some goods to Cuba and prohibited imports from Cuba. But, being a practical man, before implementing this he ordered his press secretary, Pierre Salinger, to "Get a White House car and a driver, more than one if you need them, go around Washington to all the good tobacco stores and buy up every top-grade Cuban cigar they have in stock, and bring them all back here."

From the time of Khrushchev's "secret" speech in 1956 until late 1962, it was possible in the Soviet Union to publish books like Solzhenitsyn's *One Day in the Life of Ivan Denisovich,* in which he described the horrors of the Gulag. But, in November of 1962, the first large exhibition of modern paintings in the Soviet Union was opened across from the Kremlin, and Khrushchev came to see it. As soon as he looked at the pictures, his facial expression (captured on film) changed from uncertainty to rage. As reported by William Taubman in *Khrushchev: The Man and His Era,* he shouted:

> A donkey could smear better than this with his tail. . . . The Dutch masters painted differently. You can look at their paintings through a

magnifying glass and still admire them. But your paintings just give a person constipation, if you'll pardon the expression."

After that, Krushchev restored several Stalinists to cultural posts and demanded that all artists belong to a single union that would control their activities.

When the writer Ilya Ehrenburg wrote in his memoir that he had known that innocent people were arrested under Stalin, but was afraid to speak up, Khrushchev became enraged:

> So he knew, did he? . . . If he knew, why was he silent? He makes it seem everyone was silent. Not all, comrade Ehrenburg, not all were silent, many were not silent. . . . You think it was easy for us? Just between us, just between us, the man was insane in his last years, INSANE, I tell you. A madman on the throne. Can you imagine that?. . . And you think it was easy? Our nerves were strained to the limit, and we had to drink vodka all the time. And we always had to be on the alert.

Khrushchev announced to the world that the Soviet Union had completed the Socialist stage and was entering the highest stage of human development — that of Communism. He had promised that by 1970 it would overtake the United States in the standard of living, and ordered the construction of five-story apartment blocks, without elevators and with tiny rooms and a bathroom, totaling about 500 sq. ft., which became popularly known as the "Khrushchevkas."

But as Khrushchev's plans were falling farther and farther behind, he became irritable and accused everyone of inefficiency and wastefulness. His solution for agriculture was to use more chemical fertilizers like he had seen in the United States. After visiting a kolkhoz, he concluded that much of the fertilizer was being wasted and said that this would be "inconceivable to an American farmer who pays money for fertilizers and knows that if they aren't used correctly, he will, as they say, go broke." The situation became so bad that rationing bread was seriously considered, and large quantities of grain were purchased abroad.

To encourage agricultural innovation, Khrushchev forced the Academy of Sciences to award the Lenin Prize to two followers of the agronomist Lysenko, who did not believe in genetics. Neither did Khrushchev, because as he said, "No one had ever seen a gene." When Khrushchev's daughter reminded him that no one had ever seen an atom either, he lost his temper and told her to shut up, and that if she persisted in carrying an alien ideology into his home, she'd better not "darken his door again."

Upon his return from a visit to Poland, Khrushchev asked the Moscow mayor of what material were the toilet seats in the new apartments, and when told that they were wooden, retorted: "You see. I knew it. You are spendthrifts! You've got to use plastic. I was recently in Poland. I lived in a villa. When you sit on a toilet seat like the one there, it does not feel cold. So you take a trip there, check it out and do the same in Moscow."

There was no procedure for succession in the Soviet Union, and when Khrushchev began mentioning retirement, he could not think of anyone in the Party Presidium who could take his place. For his seventieth birthday in April 1964, he was awarded the title of "Hero of the Soviet Union," and the press hailed the last ten years as a "Great Decade." But by then his colleagues could not stand his constant haranguing, and Khrushchev's protégé, the titular Head of State Brezhnev, began plotting against him. This time, in order to avoid a repetition of the failed 1957 attempt to remove Khrushchev by the Presidium of the Party alone, the plotters, before calling the meeting on October 14, 1964, secured the support of the Central Committee.

Khrushchev's ouster was not announced by the official Party newspaper *Pravda* until two days later, on October 16. On the following day, its editorial, without mentioning a name, condemned "subjectivism and drift in Communist construction, harebrained scheming, half-baked conclusions, and hasty decisions and actions divorced from reality, bragging and bluster, attraction to rule by fiat, and unwillingness to take into account what science and practical experience have already worked out."

The morning after Khrushchev was ousted, an ordinary car replaced his huge limousine, and a new security detail replaced the one that had guarded him for many years. Also, he was ordered to move into a smaller apartment, and to move from his dacha into one in a less prestigious district. Khrushchev was deeply depressed, and when a teacher asked his grandson what he was doing in retirement, the grandson said that he cried a lot. It appears that his conscience began to bother him, and when a reporter asked what he regretted about his life, he replied, "Most of all the blood. My arms are up to the elbows in blood. That is the most terrible thing that lies in my soul."

By 1966 his depression was over, and he began writing his memoir. He declined a suggestion by the KGB that Marshal Zhukov should help him, and refused to hand over the manuscript to the Presidium that had requested it. His son had hid several copies of the memoir and arranged for one copy to be smuggled out of the country. This does not mean that Khrushchev became disenchanted in Communism. While his memoir *Khrushchev Remembers* is full of self-justifications, in the last chapter "Defending the Socialist Paradise" he wrote:

> We Communists believe that capitalism is a hell in which laboring people are condemned to slavery. We are building Socialism. . . . Our way of life is undoubtedly the most progressive in the world at the present stage of humanity's development. To use the language of the Bible again, our way of life is paradise for mankind. It's not paradise in the sense that the horn of plenty is overflowing and that all you have to do is open your mouth, and you will be fed. No, we don't have that kind of paradise — at least not yet. I don't know if we ever will. But, as they say, everything is relative. And relative to the capitalist world, our way of life is a great accomplishment.

Khrushchev died in 1971 at the age of 78. That day the KGB locked his house and two men from the Central Committee came and confiscated his papers. He was buried without fanfare and the only speeches at his grave were by his son talking about him as a father, and by a coworker of his son whose father had died in the Gulag; also by a woman named Nadezhda Dimenshtein who had known him in the twenties. She had been imprisoned in the thirties and thanked Khrushchev in the name of the millions he had released from the camps.

CHAPTER 12
BREZHNEV, ANDROPOV, AND CHERNENKO

With Khrushchev's forced retirement, the plotter Leonid Brezhnev was elected by the Presidium to be the Secretary General of the Party. His biography is very similar to that of Khrushchev. He had been born into a metalworker's family, joined the Communist Youth Organization, the Komsomol, at seventeen, and the party at twenty-five. He went to a trade school, became a commissar in the army, then local party secretary and again a military commissar during World War II. In 1957 he backed Khrushchev during the "anti-party" plot, and in 1959 became a member of the Politburo, now called the Presidium.

In his memoir, published in 1995, Mikhail Gorbachev wrote: "Brezhnev came to power in October 1964 as a result of a compromise between the groups which ousted Khrushchev. He was then regarded as a rather insignificant figure, who could be easily manipulated. This was a miscalculation."

Brezhnev knew how to split the opposition and then act as a peacemaker. He never forgot any disloyalty and waited for the right moment to get even. In a 1965 speech on the twentieth anniversary of victory over Germany, Brezhnev spoke of Stalin in positive terms, and with his KGB chief Yuri Andropov strengthened censorship and control of cultural activities. Now books about the Red Terror had to be copied and circulated in secret in "sam-izdat" (self-publishing), or smuggled out and published abroad, in what was called "tam-izdat" (publishing there). When in 1970, Alexandr Solzhenitsyn was awarded the Nobel Prize in literature, he was not allowed to go to Stockholm to receive it, and in 1974 was forcibly put on a plane and escorted to Germany, from where he moved to the United States and settled in Vermont.

When the writers Yuri Daniel and Andrey Siniavsky had their books smuggled out and published abroad, they were tried and Daniel was sentenced to seven years of imprisonment and Siniavsky to five. Their arrest and the demonstrations supporting them marked the beginning of the movement for human rights in the Soviet Union. It did not question the legitimacy of the government but insisted on its strict adherence to the Soviet law and constitution that theoretically guaranteed freedom of speech, assembly, and religion.

THE PRAGUE SPRING

In 1968, the Czechoslovak President Alexander Dubcek attempted under the name of "Socialism with a Human Face" to live up to the Communist theoretical commitments. This period became popularly known as the "Prague Spring." The reforms relaxed restrictions on speech, allowed freedom of the press and the media, and travel abroad. It also limited the power of the secret police, relaxed censorship, and permitted small private businesses — all under the direction of the Communist Party. But, due to the relaxation of controls, a Social Democratic Party and several other non-Communist groups that advocated a democratic way to Socialism began to organize. For the Soviet Union, permitting a second political party was a revolt against the "dictatorship of the proletariat" that did not allow any competition to the Communist Party.

After negotiations with the Soviets had failed, Czechoslovakia was occupied by Warsaw Pact troops consisting of Soviet, Polish, Hungarian, and Bulgarian units, totaling 400,000 soldiers, 800 aircraft, 2,000 pieces of artillery, and 6,300 tanks. In comparison, in 1941 Germany had attacked the Soviet Union with only 3,580 tanks. President Dubcek asked the population not to resist, but to confuse the occupiers many towns changed their name and road signs to "Svoboda" (Freedom) or "Dubcek." One protester had set himself on fire, and his funeral ignited large demonstrations. When the Czech hockey team beat the Soviets in the world championship, half a million people staged a victory demonstration throughout the country, which the Soviets did not know how to handle.

President Dubcek and several other leaders were arrested and whisked over in handcuffs to Moscow for a confrontation with Brezhnev and his people. After three days of negotiations, Dubcek returned to Prague and was removed from office. He was replaced by Gustav Husak, who in 1954 had been sentenced to life imprisonment as "Slovak bourgeois nationalist," and had served nine years in prison. Now it was he who was sentencing hundreds of demonstrators to prison.

The justification for the invasion of Czechoslovakia was the "Brezhnev Doctrine," according to which the Soviet Union had claimed the right to interfere in the internal affairs of other countries in order to "safeguard socialism."

One of the unresolved issues that upset the Soviet leaders since the end of World War II was the refusal by Western Powers to recognize the new Soviet borders, according to which the Baltic Countries, Moldova, and Eastern Poland, became part of the Soviet Union. In 1975, in exchange for this recognition, the Soviets agreed to sign the Helsinki Final Act, which called on countries to: "Respect human rights and fundamental freedoms; including freedom of thought, conscience, religion or belief, for all without distinction as to race, sex, language or religion." These freedoms were much like those contained in the Soviet constitution, so that signing the Act was for them not a problem; they could ignore it just as they had been ignoring their constitution. However, the signing gave the Soviet dissidents an opportunity to set up Helsinki Watchdog Committees that began publicizing Soviet violations of the Act, such as imprisoning of dissidents in insane asylums.

While due to pressure from the West some limited emigration from the Soviet Union was now permitted, there were still many more people, particularly Jews, who wished to leave. In 1973, a young mathematician named Anatoly Sharansky had been refused the right to emigrate, and became, what was called a "refusenik." Because he was a member of the Moscow Helsinki Watch Committee, he was accused of spying for the United States and sentenced to thirteen years in the Gulag for divulging state secrets, such as the way dissidents were being treated. After a great deal of protest in the West, he was exchanged for two Soviet spies in 1986.

There was a joke about divulging Soviet state secrets: a man in Red Square shouted that Brezhnev was an idiot, for which he was sentenced to fifteen days for insulting Brezhnev, and to fifteen years for divulging a state secret.

In Stalin's days, a joke like this would have guaranteed a death sentence.

In his autobiography, *Fear no Evil,* Sharansky wrote about his arrest:

> Shortly after six o'clock in the evening of March 15, 1977, I was abducted by the KGB. . . . During the long months of interrogation and isolation before my trial, and for all the years that followed, my captors were determined to break me, to make me confess to crimes I had never committed, and then to parade me before the world.

FAR EAST AND AFRICA

In 1969, there were armed clashes on the border between Communist China and Soviet Union, and Chairman Mao became convinced that he needed a counterbalance to the Soviet Union. This created an opportunity for President Richard Nixon to visit China in 1972, and to establish diplomatic relations.

In addition to supplying the Vietnamese Communists with weapons, the Soviet Union subsidized Castro's Cuba, whose forces it used to penetrate Africa. When the government of the 82-year-old Emperor Haile Selassie of Ethiopia collapsed in 1974, the strongman Mengistu announced that the country would become Communist, and with Soviet and Cuban help instituted a Soviet-style government. With guidance of the Soviet KGB and East German secret police he set up his own secret police, and between February 1977 and June 1978 there were about 10,000 political assassinations in the capital Addis Ababa alone. Later, mass graves were discovered all over the country.

To rid the city of homeless children and to terrorize the population, they were murdered and their bodies displayed on sidewalks of the city. On May 17, 1977, the Swedish General Secretary of the Save the Children Fund reported:

> 1,000 children have been killed, and their bodies are left in the streets and are being eaten by wild hyenas. . . . You can see the heaped-up bodies of murdered children, most of them aged eleven to thirteen, lying in the gutter as you drive out of Addis Ababa.

In 1979 there was a massacre of Ethiopian Jews, and Israel ran an airlift to evacuate the survivors.

When in 1974, the Portuguese army, together with 400,000 refugees, had withdrawn from Angola, 7,000 Soviet and Cuban advisors moved in, and tens of thousands of people disappeared in political purges. In a typically bureaucratic way, an Amnesty International report stated that: "Their fate did not conform to internationally recognized standards of equity."

When the Portuguese left Mozambique, a similar situation developed there, and a famine caused by the collectivization of agriculture killed about 500,000 people. Altogether, it is estimated that around 1.7 million people perished in Africa due to persecutions and famines created by the Communist regimes.

THE CULT OF BREZHNEV

In 1976, Brezhnev made himself a Marshal of the Soviet Union, and the following year assumed the position of Chairman of the Supreme Soviet, thereby gaining control of both the party and the government. He revived the "personality cult" and had accumulated 114 medals of all sorts. There was a joke that when someone was told that Brezhnev was in surgery and asked whether it was again for his heart, the reply was: "No, this time it is for chest expansion to fit more medals."

To ease the shortage of housing, Brezhnev, like Khrushchev before him, ordered building of apartments. They were somewhat larger than the "Khrushchevkas," and were called "Brezhnevkas." However, the agriculture continued to lag, and large amounts of grain had to be imported. According to a joke at that time, one night Brezhnev screamed in his sleep, and when his wife asked what was the matter, he replied that he had a nightmare that the whole world became Communist. "Was not that wonderful!" said the wife. "You think so?" he said. "If this should happen, where are we going to get bread?"

To improve Soviet relations with the United States, Brezhnev In 1979 signed the SALT II treaty on arms limitation. However, when later that year to support a shaky Communist regime the Soviets invaded Afghanistan, American President Carter ordered a grain embargo and they had to scrounge for grain all over the world. To improve their image, the Soviet propaganda, both inside the country and abroad, went on a peace offensive claiming that the Soviet Union was fighting for peace. Ironically, the Russian word for peace "Mir" also means "the World," so that their slogan could be also interpreted that they were fighting to conquer the world.

It was not difficult for the Soviet propagandists to lead foreign visitors by the nose. In his book *Shadows and Whispers,* The American journalist Dusko Doder reported about the American evangelist's Billy Graham's visit to Moscow:

> That May I had a chance to see a large assortment of KGB goons, all in their Sunday best, attending church to listen to American evangelist Billy Graham. They packed the churches — young, clean-shaven men standing quietly and looking pious, as the occasion required. . . . He (Billy Graham) found the churches in Moscow packed to capacity, he said, adding, 'You would never get that in Charlotte, North Carolina.' We were all outraged by his remarks since the Soviets were so open about their opposition to religion.

*   *   *

The Brezhnev years are known as the era of stagnation: both the agriculture and the centrally controlled industry continued to decline, and there was a general shortage of everything. When the mayor of Moscow visited New York City and saw the innumerable stores overflowing with goods, he wanted to know which government office was in charge of supplying them.

In the Soviet Union, to do a project such as building a hotel, a governmental Construction Office would first have to apply to the central planners for allocation of materials and labor. But just because they were allocated did not mean that they would arrive when needed, making it impossible to get anything done on time and on budget, and the regional planners found it more efficient to contract with foreign companies for complete turn-key projects. The foreign company would do the design, bring all the materials and labor, and get the project done on time. To get anything done, the Soviet factories bypassed the central planning bureaucracy by developing an informal bartering system among themselves.

As the fear of the government decreased, people could tell critical jokes openly and dissidents could demonstrate without being shot. Even the previously holy Communist Party did not escape satire, such as:

As the Winter's cold turns to Summer's bliss,

We thank our glorious Party for this!

There was also a general decline of discipline, which was an indication that the government was losing absolute control. Dusko Doder wrote about a plant manager who was in charge of 320 people, of whom about forty did not show up for work, and another forty showed up drunk. When the manager reprimanded them, he was badly beaten, and there was nothing he could do about it.

Government corruption reached all the way to the top — Brezhnev's daughter lived like a princess with shopping trips to Paris on government airplanes — and in the apartment of her boyfriend the police found a million dollars in cash and jewels from the Tsarist era.

Toward the end of Brezhnev's eighteen-year reign, he became so feeble that two men had to support him, and he read the same page of his speeches twice. The Communist slogan "Lenin died, but his cause lives on!" was paraphrased to "Brezhnev died, but his body lives on!"

But since there was no procedure for succession, he continued in office. In the absence of leadership, the officials could do whatever they pleased, and corruption had no limits. In some Central Asian Republics, local Party leaders even set up private prisons in which they could keep their opponents without a trial. In one scandal that eventually came to light, the Soviet Republic of Uzbekistan was billing the Central Government for cotton shipments which exceeded the number of available railroad cars that could have delivered them.

Even after Brezhnev had a stroke in March of 1982, there was still no official way to remove him and he ruled the country until his death of a heart attack in November. He lay in state for four days, while a symphony orchestra in black tie played classical music. On the day of the funeral, all classes were canceled and the roads into Moscow were closed. But even after he died, the jokes did not cease: presumably, the Politburo could not decide where to bury him — they considered Lenin's mausoleum too grand, but the Kremlin wall, where the other leaders were buried, seemed not grand enough. They finally decided on the Tomb of the Unknown Soldier, because it was not known whether Brezhnev had been a soldier.

ANDROPOV AND THE KGB TAKE OVER

After Brezhnev's death, Yuri Andropov, the sixty-eight-year-old head of the KGB, became the new Secretary General of the Party. He had attended the Water Transport Technical College and joined the Komsomol at sixteen and the Party at twenty-five. He became the secretary of a regional branch of the party, and during the war was a commissar with the partisan guerillas behind the German lines, making sure that the partisans did not become infected by any non-Communist ideas.

In 1954 Andropopv became Ambassador to Hungary, and during the 1956 Hungarian uprising it was he who convinced Khrushchev to suppress it by military force. He tricked the Hungarian leaders to come to negotiations at the Soviet headquarters and had them arrested and shot. With this experience, he was appointed to keep the Communist parties in the satellite countries in line and in 1967 became the head of the KGB and directed the suppression of the Prague Spring. There was also a strong suspicion that under his leadership the KGB had been involved in the attempt to assassinate Pope John Paul, and, according to rumors, one of his plans was to maim the ballet dancer Rudolf Nureyev, who had defected to the West.

Andropov was obsessed with "destruction of dissidence in all its forms," and insisted that "the struggle for human rights was part of a wide-ranging imperialist plot to undermine the foundations of the Soviet State." He tried to combat corruption and dismissed eighteen ministers and thirty-seven First Party Secretaries of the Soviet Republics and Regions. Also, he began criminal procedures of the highest party and state officials, like the appointed-by-Brezhnev Minister of Interior who had provided for his family sixteen Mercedes and Volvo cars, and was appropriating goods confiscated by the Customs Office. In Uzbekistan, Andropov had KGB helicopters fly over the cotton fields and assess the harvest, so that the local powers could not bill the central government for phantom deliveries as they had done in the past. Like many of his colleagues, Andropov had written poetry, and in one of his poems wrote that it is not the power that corrupts the people, but the people that corrupt the power.

In his book *Lenin's Tomb*, American correspondent David Remnick, wrote that Andropov "frightened the worst elements in the apparatus so badly that a series of ranking officials in Brezhnev's old circle shot, gassed, or otherwise did away with themselves."

When in response to the deployment of Soviet medium-range missiles in Soviet satellite countries in Eastern Europe, United States had deployed its Pershing missiles in Western Europe, Andropov refused to negotiate a compromise, calculating that the American and international peace movements would force the U.S. to capitulate. To encourage the peace movements, Andropov, who believed in the power of propaganda, announced that the Soviets were halting development of space weapons, but did not offer any means of verification. He made headlines around the world when, upon receiving a letter from an American school girl calling for peace, he invited her to visit the Soviet Union.

When in September 1983, the South Korean jetliner with 269 people on board strayed over Soviet waters and was shot down by a fighter plane, the Soviets found its black box but kept it secret until in 1992 when President of Russia Boris Yeltsin admitted that they had it.

For the last two months of his life, Andropov did not get out of bed, but, unlike his predecessors, he recommended his protégé Gorbachev as his successor. However, the former Brezhnev cronies in the Politburo were not interested in replacing one corruption fighter with another and ignored Andropov's wish.

According to a former KGB subordinate, in governing the Soviet Union Andropov substituted the KGB for the Communist Party. His contribution to the country was in openly admitting the dismal performance of the economy in contrast with Khrushchev's assertion that the Soviet economy would surpass that of the United States. Also, the Party program for the 1980s claimed that there would be so much food that workers would be fed free of charge in factory canteens, children would get free clothing and books, and all citizens would have rent-free housing and utilities, as well as free transportation and two-month vacations per year. The discrepancy between this rosy picture and the reality was so obvious that no one could believe any official pronouncements.

When Andropov died on February 9, 1984, and, as for Brezhnev, a four-day period of national mourning was decreed again, and on the stage of the hall where he lay in state surrounded by flowers, a complete symphony orchestra in black tailcoats played classical music. The funeral cortege halted in the middle of Red Square, and the open coffin was placed on a red-draped bier facing the Lenin Mausoleum as if before being buried near the Kremlin wall, one corpse was taking leave from another.

THE PARTY RETAKES POWER

On February 13, 1984, disregarding Andropov's wish that Gorbachev take his place, the Politburo elected the 73-year-old Konstantin Chernenko to be the Secretary General of the Party. Two months later it made him also Chairman of the Presidium of the Supreme Soviet, which gave him the power to once again subordinate the KGB to the Party.

Chernenko had joined the Komsomol at eighteen and the Party at twenty. After serving as a border guard, he became director of the regional Agitation and Propaganda Department — a doublespeak title for a job that varnishes the truth.

Chernenko had met Brezhnev in 1956 and became his chief of staff and a member of the Central Committee. For twenty years he every day signed hundreds of party documents, and one of his duties was to monitor the telephone and wiretapping devices in offices of the top party members. He was what they call a true apparatchik.

At Andropov's funeral, Chernenko could barely read the eulogy — he spoke rapidly, swallowed his words, kept coughing, and repeatedly stopped to wipe his lips and forehead. Climbing the stairs, he needed the help of two bodyguards. A joke about the announcement of his election said: "Today, due to bad health and without regaining consciousness, Konstantin Ustinovich Chernenko took up the duties of Secretary General."

Chernenko represented return to Brezhnev's policies. According to a former Soviet diplomat, Chernenko was "demanding, rude, authoritarian and arrogant, but also a pragmatic businessman and a master of wheeling and dealing on the Central Committee." He proposed reforms in education and propaganda, which in his mind were probably the same thing, and replaced the chief of the General Staff who advocated less spending on consumer goods and more on weapons.

In foreign policy, he negotiated a trade pact with China and resumed arms-control talks with the United States. Because the United States had boycotted the 1980 Summer Olympics in Moscow when the Soviet Union invaded Afganistan, the Soviets in turn boycotted the 1984 Olympics in Los Angeles.

By the end of 1984, Chernenko could not leave the hospital, and the Politburo was affixing a facsimile of his signature. He died on March 10, 1985, after only thirteen months in office. His predecessor, Andropov, had been in office somewhat less than 16 months. The frequency of the leader's funerals gave rise to a joke that the reason sick old men were being elected, was that the government must have been selling season tickets for best places to view their funerals in the Red Square. When President Reagan was asked why he did not have a summit meeting with the

Soviet leaders, he replied that he would have liked to have one, but they kept dying on him.

Chernenko's death was reported in an unusual manner: instead of his obituary on the front page of the papers, there was a report on the election of Mikhail Gorbachev, with his large portrait and biography. The announcement of Chernenko's death and his obituary were on page two. When, according to custom, his successor Gorbachev opened Chernenko's safe, it contained a packet of personal papers and large bundles of money.

Upon Chernenko's death, the Politburo members could not again appoint another sick old man and needed someone energetic, young and reliable, who could initiate the needed reforms, and Gorbachev fit these requirements. Even though he was not well-known by the people, his election was greeted with joy that finally, the younger generation was taking over, and continuity and stability could be counted upon. After Chernenko's funeral at noon, Gorbachev presented himself at the 2 p.m. reception for the representatives of more than 120 countries and then held private meetings with several top leaders.

≋

CHAPTER 13

WHO WAS GORBACHEV?

Mikhail Gorbachev was born in 1931 and grew up on a collective farm in the South of Russia. As a youngster, he operated a harvester just as did his father. No one in his immediate family was a Party member, and his paternal grandfather, Andrei, was accused of hoarding forty pounds of grain during the 1931-1932 famine, and spent nine years in the Gulag. Gorbachev recalled his grandmother whispering about the hardships of being a family of an "enemy of the people." His grandfather returned home just before World War II, and raised Mikhail, whose father was drafted into the army.

Upon graduating from high school, Gorbachev went to Moscow to study law, which he might have chosen in order to right the injustices done to his family. He joined the Komsomol, without which it was impossible to advance, and was soon elected a Komsomol organizer. As described by Doder and Branson in their book *Gorbachev: Heretic in the Kremlin*, Gorbachev demonstrated his ability as a politician when the night before the election he got his competitor drunk, and then denounced his behavior. After a year in college, he wrote to his wife:

> I am so depressed at the situation here.... How disgusting my surroundings are here. Especially the manner of life by the local (party) bosses. The

acceptance of convention, subordination, with everything predetermined, the open impudence of officials and the arrogance.

In spite of such low opinion of the Party, he joined it at the age of twenty-one because, again, this was the only way to advance in the Soviet Union.

In 1966, Gorbachev was part of a Soviet group invited by a leftist French businessman, who paid their expenses, to visit France. He and his wife Raissa made a 3,000-mile tour of the country and saw the life of non-collectivized small farmers and private shopkeepers. A year later, they toured Italy. These trips must have greatly influenced his understanding of the West.

When in 1971 Gorbachev became the First Party Secretary in his home region, he introduced an incentive system for selected farmers in a local kolkhoz. They were allocated parcels of land that became their responsibility, and were paid according to what they had produced. Gorbachev claimed that these farmers harvested 20 to 30 percent more than others, and advocated an increase in private plots which, while occupying only about 3 percent of the total arable land, produced about one-quarter of all fruit and vegetables.

As a delegate to the Party Congress in Moscow, Gorbachev voted that Stalin's body be removed from the Lenin Mausoleum because of his "abuse of power, mass repression of honest Soviet people, and other actions." When the Central Committee member in charge of agriculture, who had been severely criticized, died of a heart attack in 1978 (or, according to rumors, committed suicide), Andropov appointed Gorbachev to take his place.

The harvest that year was an all-time record, but the subsequent years were disastrous, and imports of grain increased tenfold. Large grain losses were due to negligence and lack of storage facilities. Also, even though the country produced every year 550,000 tractors, their number available to the collective farms was not increasing due to mishandling and lack of parts. In a TV interview, a tractor plant manager showed hundreds of new tractors sitting in a lot, each missing one belt that had not been delivered on time.

WHAT WERE GLASNOST AND PERESTROIKA?

Gorbachev realized that the stagnation in industry and agriculture could not go on much longer and that drastic action was urgently needed. In his book *Perestroika: New Thinking for Our Country and the World*, he wrote:

> Propaganda of success — real or imagined — was gaining the upper hand. Eulogizing and servility were encouraged; the needs and opinions of ordinary working people, of the people at large, were ignored. . . . Alcoholism, drug addiction, and crime were growing.

Gorbachev knew that to reform the economy, he would have to reform the political system first, and that in order for people to accept the reforms, they needed to believe that they were being listened to, and that their cooperation made a difference. To achieve this, he needed to give them the freedom to express themselves, to be able to obtain information, and to participate in creation of new approaches. But he still wanted the reforms to be carried out under the leadership of the Communist Party, which he also wanted to reform and save, rather than destroy.

He called this new approach *glasnost*. The word *glas* is a form of the Russian word for voice, meaning "sounding off," that implies openness and transparency. While glasnost for him meant open and honest discussion, it also required orderly and responsible public participation, and he believed in the good sense of the Russian people to do the right thing if given a chance, even if it required some sacrifice.

To revive agriculture, Gorbachev intended to restore the family farms, and have the collective farms support them with equipment and marketing. However, the great majority of the Russian people did not jump at the opportunity to become self-sufficient. Having lived for three generations under a government that had told them what to do, and how and when to do it, Soviet people did not know how to respond to incentives and to assume responsibility for their own welfare.

But they did not lose their sense of humor, and, as always, came up with a joke. This one was about a peasant who found an old lamp, and as he tried to clean it, a genie appeared and offered to grant him anything he wished. After a long hesitation, the peasant said: "Well, my neighbor has five cows, but I have only one." "Would you also want to have five cows?" asked the genie. "No," said the peasant. "That would be too much work, I want four of his cows to die."

To improve the economy, Gorbachev consulted many experts from whom he expected informed advice and not the usual sloganeering. Gorbachev's adviser on the United States, Georgy Arbatov, wrote (as quoted by Doder in *Gorbachev*):

He likes to call in experts and grill them on details on topics he feels uncertain about. He will forgive you once or even twice if you are unable to brief him well. But after that, he will be ruthless and just cut you off. He does not like to waste time.

Gorbachev was outspoken and blunt, and after a confrontational meeting with American Senator Ted Kennedy, he was advised that he might benefit from reading Dale Carnegie's book *How to Win Friends and Influence People.* He ordered it to be translated, and after that the American ambassador said he found him a changed man:

He did not begin with a long lecture, as he used to. Instead, in a very flattering way he asked them questions, got them to pose their own questions, and then in a very nice sort of way answered them. He was able to make all the points he wanted to make, but they were flattered and charmed by the idea that he wanted them to ask questions and express views.

Gorbachev called the proposed reforms of the economy *perestroika,* meaning "reconstruction", and wrote:

Perestroika is an urgent necessity arising from the profound processes of development in our socialist society. This society is ripe for change. It has been yearning for it. Any delay at the beginning of perestroika could have led to an exacerbated internal situation in the near future, which, to put it bluntly, would have been fraught with serious social, economic, and political crisis.

The goal of Perestroika was to transform the government-controlled economy into a "democratic economy." To achieve this, Gorbachev passed *The Law on Socialist Enterprise,* which recognized profit as the mechanism for efficiency and incentive for production of things people would want to buy. This was a revolutionary step — before that, *profit* was considered a capitalist word and the prices for every item were set by the government, and were frequently unrelated to cost. According to this law, the government would retain control of heavy industry but leave small enterprises to private initiative.

His *Law on Cooperatives* permitted private ownership of businesses in twenty-nine fields as long as they employed only family members. This action legalized the small restaurants, shoe repairmen, tailors, plumbers, electricians, language tutors, etc., that had been illegally operating privately anyway. Until then, the way to get something repaired was either to call for a repairman from a government-controlled cooperative and wait forever, or to find a moonlighter who could also bring the needed materials that he would steal from his workplace.

As for everything else, there was a joke on this subject about a man who ordered a car and was told that it would be delivered in precisely a year from the order date. He looked at his calendar and asked if it would be in the morning or in the afternoon. When the salesman asked what difference it would make a year from now, he replied that it would, because that afternoon the plumber will be coming to fix a leak.

In general, the public's attitude toward government was cynical — the big shots were riding in their limousines, shopping in special stores where everything was available, and living in their dachas, while the common people lived in communal apartments, frequently with a family to a room. In the workplace, the attitude was, "they pretend to be paying us, and we pretend to be working."

To break the grip on power by the entrenched party bureaucracy that kept appointing one another without any opposition, in 1987 Gorbachev made another revolutionary proposal that elections have more than one candidate for each seat, and that non-party candidates also be eligible for government positions.

One of the reasons for the economic problems was widespread alcoholism. Gorbachev made it a priority to fight it, and called in his Health Minister to report on the state of alcoholism in the country. When the minister gave him platitudes, Gorbachev told him: "We did not ask you to come here and tell us that alcoholism is bad; we know that. You better come back and tell us what we can do about it."

What he could do about it, was raise the price of vodka and limit its distribution. Factories that made the bottles for vodka were ordered to destroy their molds, so that when later these restrictions were lifted, vodka had to be sold in soft-drink bottles. This was a very unpopular move, and it earned Gorbachev the title of "Secretary of Mineral Water." The consequence of this action was a decrease in tax revenue, which was expected, but an unexpected consequence was severe shortage of sugar that people began using to make moonshine.

When at the summit meeting in 1985, Gorbachev and Reagan discovered that they both had a sense of humor, they began swapping jokes. Gorbachev's was that when due to his actions the lines for vodka became very long, one frustrated man, after standing several hours in line, screamed that he was going to the Kremlin to kill Gorbachev. When after some time he returned and was asked whether he did it, he replied: "No, the line there is even longer than the one here."

One of Reagan's jokes was that when an American bragged to a Russian about freedom of speech in the United States and said that he could stand in Times Square shouting that Reagan was an idiot and nothing would happen to him, the Russian replied: "Big deal! I could stand in the Red Square and shout that Reagan is an idiot, and nothing would happen to me either."

Reagan, who had been waiting for a Soviet leader with whom he could talk, wrote in his diary:

> Starting with Brezhnev, I'd dreamed of personally going one-on-one with a Soviet leader because I thought we might be able to accomplish things our countries' diplomats could not do because they did not have the authority. . . . Until Gorbachev, I never got an opportunity to try out my idea.

In 1985, the Soviet Union had suspended deployment in Europe of their middle-range missiles, and at the Geneva summit meeting with Reagan, Gorbachev proposed that both countries cut their nuclear arsenals in half. However, they could not agree on a method of verification, about which Reagan said in Russian: "Doveriay no Proveriay" – "Trust but Verify."

On April 26, 1986, a nuclear power plant exploded in a Ukrainian town called Chernobyl. The released radiation was ten times greater than that from the bomb at Hiroshima, but Gorbachev did not follow his announced principle of openness and was silent for eight days. When heavy radiation was detected in Scandinavia and even in Scotland, the accident, in addition to being a human and economic disaster, became also a disaster in international public relations.

Because of the attempted cover-up, children continued to play in the radioactive dust, absorbing radiation equivalent to 1,000 chest X-rays. Also, the Deputy Prime Minister delayed ordering evacuation, saying that a panic would be worse than the radiation.

As a result of the meltdown, thirty-one workers died immediately, and 200 suffered radiation sickness. More than 600,000 workers took part in the cleanup and 100,000 people were eventually evacuated from the area. Many local residents, especially the elderly, did not believe the government warnings, and because they could not see the radiation, returned to their homes and ate contaminated food. Many children in the area were born with birth defects.

Chernobyl is the Russian word for Wormwood, the name of a bush with bitter oily leaves, and an interesting prophecy is found in the Bible, Revelations 8:10-11: "A great star shot from the sky, flaming like a torch; and it fell on a third of the rivers and springs. The name of the star is called Wormwood, and a third of the water turned to Wormwood, and men in great numbers died of the water because it was poisoned."

With the Soviet economy still not improving, Gorbachev was eager to come to an agreement on arms control, which would have permitted him to cut the military budget and spend more money on the economy. He looked forward to the next summit meeting with Reagan but, just then, a Soviet official at the United Nations in New York was arrested for trying to buy technical information, and was charged with espionage. In retaliation, the KGB arrested an American newsman named Nicholas Daniloff, whom they framed by having their agent — who claimed to be a dissident — hand Daniloff a letter to deliver to the U.S. consulate. Daniloff was accused of espionage, and the Soviets made an offer to trade him for the Soviet spy. The United States refused the offer because it would have meant that the two cases were equal.

To sweeten the deal, the Soviets offered in addition to Daniloff to free the famous dissident Yuri Orlov, who had been in prison for nine years. This was accepted, and at a summit meeting in Reykjavik an agreement was reached to limit the number of nuclear warheads and intermediate-range nuclear missiles. However, President Reagan did not agree to limit research on the Strategic Defense Initiative (SDI), the much-ridiculed anti-missile missiles program, nicknamed "Star Wars" by its detractors in the media. Commenting on the SDI, Gorbachev's closest advisor accused the United States of trying to force the Soviet Union to arm itself to an economic death, which was actually Reagan's intention. Shortly after the Soviet Union collapsed, the former Soviet Chief of Staff said in a television interview that one of the causes of the Soviet Union's collapse was its inability to compete with the "Star Wars" development program.

On June 12, 1987, President Reagan visited West Berlin and challenged Gorbachev to tear down the Berlin Wall. A year later, in 1988, Gorbachev announced the end of the Brezhnev Doctrine, according to which the Soviet Union had claimed the right to interfere in other countries to save their Communist governments. It was replaced by the so-called Sinatra "I did it my way" doctrine, that would allow the Soviet satellite countries to determine their own affairs. Also, on July 6, 1989, Gorbachev told the Council of Europe in Strasburg that "Any interference in the internal affairs, or any attempt to limit the sovereignty of another state, friend, ally, or another, would be inadmissible," for which in 1990 he was awarded the Nobel Peace Prize.

THE BEGINNING OF THE END

The fall of the Berlin Wall began with a mistake. On November 9, 1989, an East German newsman asked a member of the Communist government what would happen now, with the Brezhnev Doctrine no longer in efffect, if an East Berliner wanted to visit West Berlin. Instead of saying that permission would be granted, the official misspoke and said that he could go. When the news that people from East Berlin could now go to West Berlin was flashed, large crowds gathered at the checkpoints and in one of them, an East German guard opened the gate. The crowds rushed to the west side of the Berlin Wall and soon began tearing it down.

When the East German Communist rulers asked the Soviets to intervene, they were told that the German reunification was their internal affair. Poland and Hungary supported Gorbachev's actions, and one after another the satellite countries held elections that peacefully ousted their Communist regimes and introduced multi-party systems and free economies. Only in Romania, the hated dictator Ceausescu had ordered troops to fire on demonstrating students. When masses of workers joined the demonstrations, Ceausescu fled, but was caught and executed together with his equally universally hated wife.

In the Soviet Union, in spite of Gorbachev's reforms, the economy continued to deteriorate, and by the end of the 1980s food ration cards for meat and sugar had to be reintroduced. From 1985, when Gorbachev came to power, to 1990, the national debt rose from zero to $120 billion and the gold reserves dwindled from 2,000 to 200 tons.

The animosities between various nationalities the KGB had previously suppressed by shooting the nationalists, now began to re-emerge. In the capital of Azerbaijan, Baku, there was a pogrom on Armenians who lived there, and there were skirmishes between ethnic Armenians and Azerbaijanis for contested territory. Tanks had to be sent to restore order, but the fighting lasted until 1996, when the Armenians had prevailed. Also, when Gorbachev replaced the corrupt Secretary of the Party in Kazakhstan with a non-Kazakh, there were riots in the capital Alma Ata, in which several policemen and many rioters were killed.

In 1989, the first free election since 1917 was held in the Soviet Union. It was an election to the Congress of People's Deputies, in which for the first time in seventy-two years more than one candidate could compete for each seat, and candidates did not have to be members of the Communist Party. As a result, many Communist candidates were defeated, and some nationalists, who wanted the fifteen republics to become independent countries, were elected.

Each of the fifteen republics constituting the Soviet Union had its own Congress and its own branch of the Communist Party, but all were controlled from Moscow by the Communist Party of the Soviet Union and none had its own president. But on June 12, 1990, the Russian Republic elected Boris Yeltsin to be its president and he announced that the laws of the Russian Republic would supersede those of the Soviet Union. This created a conflict with Gorbachev, because Moscow, in addition to being the capital of the Soviet Union, now became also the capital of the Russian Republic and, in addition to having become the home of two presidents, it also became the home of two Congresses that did not see eye to eye.

WHO WAS YELTSIN?

Boris Yeltsin was born in 1931 in Western Siberia. In 1934 his father had been convicted of anti-Soviet agitation and sentenced to hard labor in the Gulag. His mother was a seamstress. As a young boy, he and his friends stole a hand grenade from an army supply depot, and it exploded when they tried to disassemble it. He lost a thumb and an index finger on his left hand.

When he became president, Yeltsin found his father's file in the KGB archives, and learned that both his father and an uncle had been accused of "anti-Soviet agitation among workers, having as their goal the demoralization of the working class and sowing dissatisfaction with the existing law and order. Exploiting the difficulties in the provision of food and supplies, they tried to create ill will spreading provocative rumors. . . ."

In 1961, Yeltsin joined the Communist Party and in 1976 was promoted to the post of First Secretary of the Party of the Sverdlovsk region in Siberia, which put him in charge of one of the most important industrial areas. He later said, "I sincerely believed in the ideals of justice propagated by the party, and just as sincerely joined the party." But in 1989, two years before the Soviet Union disintegrated, he said, "Let's not talk about Communism. Communism was just an idea, just pie in the sky."

While he was the party boss in Sverdlovsk, a flood undermined the shore of a river and washed out a mass grave of gulag prisoners. There were so many frozen bodies floating down the river that they created a logjam.

At some point Yeltsin came to the attention of Gorbachev, who in 1985 brought him to Moscow, appointed him First Secretary of the Moscow Party Committee, and put him in charge of eliminating corruption in the local party organization. Yeltsin publicly attacked the bureaucrats, fired and reshuffled his staff several times, and, portraying himself as a reformer and populist, used public busses instead of limousines. In his book *Yeltsin*, Leon Aron quotes him as saying:

> It is hard for me to explain to the factory workers why, in the seventh year of [Gorbachev's] political power, [the worker] is obliged to stand in line for sausages, in which there is more starch than meat, while on our table there is sturgeon, caviar and all sort of delicacies easily acquired from a place which he cannot even approach.

The secret of Yeltsin's popularity was that he voiced what people were really thinking. He became a member of the Central Committee and eventually a member of the Politburo. However, he remained very blunt and began to criticize the slow pace of reforms and accused Gorbachev of developing a personality cult. His frustration reached a point where he did something that had never been done before: he resigned from the Politburo.

Gorbachev called him immature and irresponsible and relieved him of his positions. After his demotion Yeltsin was hospitalized and there were rumors that he had tried to commit suicide. However, he was allowed to remain in Moscow and was given a job as deputy chairman of the State Construction Committee, but was not given anything to do. In his book *The Struggle for Russia*, Yeltsin wrote: "Few people know what torture it is to sit in the dread silence of an office, in a complete vacuum, subconsciously waiting for something. For this telephone with the state seal to ring. Or not."

But he remained popular, and in March 1989 was elected as a delegate from Moscow to the Congress of People's Deputies of the Russian Republic. The Congress in turn elected the Supreme Soviet of the Russian Republic, and two months later the Supreme Soviet elected Yeltsin as its chairman. He was supported by both the democratic members who advocated implementation of reforms, and by conservative members who wanted stability. On June 12, 1990, Boris Yeltsin was elected President of the Russian Republic.

In January 1991, the pro-independence movement in Latvia staged a large demonstration for independence and the Soviet army opened fire and killed fourteen people. Yeltsin immediately flew to the neighboring Estonia and signed a treaty of cooperation between the Russian Republic and the three Baltic republics: Estonia, Latvia and Lithuania, that demonstrated independence of the foreign policy of the Russian Republic from that of the Soviet Union. Upon return to Moscow he made a speech on television: "It has become very obvious that while preserving the word perestroika, Gorbachev does not want to undergo perestroika in reality, but merely wants to preserve the system, preserve the harshly centralized government, and not give independence to republics, Russia above all. . . . I call for his immediate resignation."

The differences between the President of the Soviet Union Gorbachev and the President of the Russian Republik Yeltsin, were irreconcilable. Gorbachev wanted to preserve the Soviet Union as a single country with a central government in control of foreign policy and of the armed forces. He called it the FEDERATION OF INDEPENDENT REPUBLICS.

Yeltsin wanted to replace the Soviet Union by a COMMONWEALTH OF INDEPENDENT STATES, each state with its own armed forces and its own foreign policy, with a figurehead president who, in Yeltsin's words, would function something like the Queen of England.

Both ideas were strongly opposed by traditional Communists, who feared that the independent Republics would weaken the Empire and even, horror of horrors, might have more than one political party.

To give his idea legitimacy, on March 17, 1991, Gorbachev arranged a referendum in which the majority voted for the Federation as proposed by him, but in which six of the fifteen republics did not participate.

CHAPTER 14
THE END OF THE EMPIRE

The following is based on the events as they were described by the *Washington Post* correspondent David Remnick in his book *Lenin's Tomb*, which has been paraphrazed here.

When Gorbachev announced that on August 20, 1991, he and the heads of the Republics would be signing a new Treaty of the Union which would give the Republics greater autonomy, his opponents decided to act.

Two months before this date, on June 20, 1991, the U.S. Secretary of State James Baker had informed the Soviet Foreign Minister that he had intelligence about a possible coup to unseat Gorbachev. But Gorbachev did not take this warning seriously.

On August 16, Gorbachev went with his family to Crimea for their summer vacation, but he planned to return to Moscow on the 20th to sign the Union Treaty. Therefore, the conspirators could not wait any longer, and on August 18 they launched a coup. They set up the Committee for the State of Emergency, the legal justification for which would be that the President was incapacitated, and the nation was in crisis. Next, they sent a team to the Crimea to isolate Gorbachev by disconnecting the presidential communication system and keeping Gorbachev under house arrest. Also, they ordered 250,000 handcuffs and

300,000 arrest forms. The KGB cleared out a secret bunker in the Lubianka prison, and recalled all its men from their vacations.

Gorbachev's compound in Crimea was new and had an elaborate communication system manned at all times by several operators, and he was very surprised when he picked up a phone and it was dead. Even the phone of the commander in chief that no one was allowed to touch, was dead. He knew then that something was seriously wrong.

Soon five men arrived from Moscow: two from the Politburo, a general, a man from the industry, and Gorbachev's own assistant. They told Gorbachev that he had to choose either to go along with the state of emergency or resign and if he agreed to the state of emergency, they would take care of arresting its opponents. They also brought a list of the members of the State of Emergency Committee, on which he found names of people he had appointed himself, like the minister of defense and his own chief of staff.

Gorbachev replied: "You are nothing but adventurers and traitors, and you will pay for this. I don't care what happens to you, but you will destroy the country. Only those who want to commit suicide can now suggest a totalitarian regime in the country. You are pushing it to a civil war."

When they left, Gorbachev said: "I was always an opponent of such measures, not for moral and political reasons, but because in the history of our country they have always led to the death of hundreds, thousands, and millions. And we need to get away from that forever."

Upon return to Moscow, the delegation went to the Kremlin and told the conspirators that Gorbachev had "either a heart attack or something." Since Gorbachev had refused to cooperate, they needed another president who would sign the State of Emergency decree. They asked the vice president, Gennadi Yanayev, to join them as an appointed President, but he wanted to meet with Gorbachev first. They could have selected one of their own, but they wanted to make the coup more legitimate by having a disappointed Gorbachev supporter. When they then asked the Foreign Minister, Aleksandr Bessmertnykh, to become president, he asked to see a medical report.

When someone inquired about the detailed plans for the State of Emergency, no one could tell him, because they did not exist. When at four in the morning on August 19, Vice President Yanayev finally agreed to become President and sign the emergency decree, the Minister of Defense Dmitri Yazov sent a coded telegram ordering alert of all military units and occupation of Moscow. By seven a.m. the prime minister was so drunk that he needed a doctor.

The news went on the air at six a.m.:

> We are addressing you at a grave, critical hour for the future of the Motherland and our people. A mortal danger has come to loom large over our great Motherland. . . . The country is sinking into the quagmire of violence and lawlessness. Never before in national history has the propaganda of sex and violence assumed such a scale, threatening the health and lives of future generations. Millions of people are demanding measures against the octopus of crime and glaring immorality.

By 9 a.m., tanks had surrounded the Russian White House (the seat of the Parliament), and soldiers replaced the flag of the Russian Republic with that of the Soviet Union. They tried to arrest Yeltsin, but having heard the broadcast he had rushed to the White House, from where on a small radio station he called for a general strike, and for people to come to defend the White House. Then he went out, climbed on one of the tanks and told the crowd:

> The legally elected president of the country has been removed from power ... We are dealing with a right-wing reactionary, anti-constitutional coup d'etat. . . . Accordingly, we proclaim all decisions and decrees of this committee to be illegal. We demand a return of the country to normal constitutional development.

Then, a general and a colonel, also standing on tanks, called on "My brother officers, soldiers, and sailors, do not act against your own people, against your fathers, brothers, and sisters."

By the end of the day, some 25,000 people assembled at the White House and began building barricades to protect it. Gorbachev listened on a transistor radio and his wife Raissa, afraid that he might be poisoned, made sure he ate only the food that was eaten by the guards.

In Moscow, the Emergency Committee could not decide if it should order an attack on the White House to arrest Yeltsin. Some army units were loyal to the Russian Republic rather than to the Soviet Union and were ready to shoot down assault helicopters if they attacked the White House. Even the KGB forces were not fully reliable. Also, women formed the front line at the barricades with signs: "Soviet Soldiers: Don't Shoot Your Mothers." While the barricades did not present an obstacle for the Special Forces, storming them would have resulted in a bloodbath that the emergency committee did not want.

During the night, three protesters were shot dead and some tanks were set on fire by Molotov cocktails. The only foreign leaders who expressed support for the putsch were Iraq's Saddam Hussein, Libya's Muammar Gaddafi, and Cuba's Fidel Castro.

The revolt ended just as suddenly as it began. At the meeting of the emergency committee, some of the members insisted that they had the support of the majority, but Vice President Yanayev said the telegrams he received were saying just the opposite. Since the conspirators did not expect so much resistance, they did not know what to do when it happened, and at 3:00 a.m. on August 21, they decided to end the revolt. The KGB chief called the White House and told Yeltsin's assistant: "It's okay now. You can go to sleep," and by 1:00 p.m. the troops were withdrawn from the city. According to a Russian saying appropriate for this occasion, "Sometimes the thunder comes not from a cloud but from a pile of manure."

Gorbachev did not think it was safe to fly back to Moscow in his presidential plane, and instead flew in the plane of the Yeltsin's Russian Republic. He was told of Yeltsin's part in defeating the coup and was reminded that the conspirators were all his own men, to which he replied: "I had complete confidence in the people around me, and I relied on them. My gullibility undermined me. On the other hand, it's probably good to trust people, but not to this extent."

Gorbachev's military adviser, Sergey Akhromeyev, was found in his office hanging from a noose. In the suicide note to his family, he wrote: "I cannot live when my Fatherland is dying and all that I have made my life's work is being destroyed." The KGB chief shot his wife and then himself; the official in charge of finances of the

Central Committee jumped to his death from his apartment window, and there were rumors of at least fifteen more suicides that were not officially reported.

Although Gorbachev was restored to his position, his power had been weakened, and no one heeded his command: the popular support swung over to Yeltsin. Gorbachev continued to defend the Communist Party and talked about "renewing the Party," but his adviser told him: "The Party is dead. Why can't you see that? Talk about its renewal is senseless. It's like offering first aid to a corpse!"

Now Yeltsin was in his glory. He had never forgiven Gorbachev for dismissing him from his post as First Secretary of the Moscow Party in 1987, when Gorbachev had him leave his hospital bed and stand before the Moscow City Party organization for hours of denunciations. To humiliate Gorbachev, during a televised session of the Russian Parliament, Yeltsin forced him to read aloud a transcript of the August 19 Council of Ministers meeting, at which most of Gorbachev's nominees pledged their support to the coup. Then Yeltsin said, "Shall we now sign a decree suspending the activities of the Russian Communist Party?" implying that it was the party leadership that had tried to overthrow the government.

The beaten Gorbachev did not sign the suspension of party activities, but on August 24, he resigned as Secretary General of the Communist Party and dissolved its Central Committee. However, he did not abandon his idea of some kind of Federal Union, and in September 1991 assembled in the Kremlin the Congress of People's Deputies. Russia, Estonia, Latvia, Lithuania, Moldova, and Georgia, considered themselves by then to be independent and did not participate. The other nine republics agreed to establish a new, decentralized Union in which Moscow would retain some functions.

In November 1991, Yeltsin outlawed the Communist Party in the Russian Republic on the grounds that it was not a political party but a "special mechanism for the creation and realization of political power." This was unimaginable. The Communist Party had been the brain and the sinew of the state for almost seventy-five years; it penetrated and controlled every aspect of life and three generations of people could not even imagine living under a different political system.

Now that the Bolshevik Era was coming to an end, people began topling statues of the old Bolsheviks, including those of the "Iron" Felix Dzerzhinsky who in 1917 founded the Cheka — the brutal secret police. The Museum of the Revolution put up a display honoring resistance to the coup, and the Lenin Museum closed down "for repairs."

In an article in the *New Yorker* magazine, David Remnick described the inglorious end of the Soviet Empire. On December 7 and 8, 1991, in a forest near Minsk, Boris Yeltsin secretly met with Leonid Kravchuk and Stanislav Shushkevich, the presidents of the Ukrainian and the Belorussian Republics. They toasted one another with vodka, and while their aides worked on a statement, went to a local bathhouse.

The world-shaking death certificate of the Union of Soviet Socialist Republics (U.S.S.R.), signed by the three men at 2:17 p.m. on Sunday, December 8, 1991, read:

WE, THE PEOPLE OF BELARUS, THE RUSSIAN FEDERATION, AND UKRAINE, AS ORIGINATORS OF THE U.S.S.R. ON THE BASIS OF THE UNION TREATY OF 1922, CONFIRM THAT THE U.S.S.R. AS A SUBJECT OF

INTERNATIONAL LAW AND GEOPOLITICAL
REALITY CEASES ITS EXISTENCE.

Yeltsin delivered the good news not to Gorbachev, but to American President George H. W. Bush. It was the President of Belarus Shushkevich who called Gorbachev and told him that the Soviet Union no longer existed. Gorbachev, the President of the Soviet Union, then asked: "What happens to me now?"

Having become a president without a country, there was nothing left for Gorbachev to do but to resign, which he did. He was like the engineer at Chernobyl who wanted to improve the nuclear reactor, only for it to go out of control and explode.

However, unlike the Chernobyl reactor, the Bolshevik Empire ended not with a bang, but with a whimper. **The Bolsheviks, who in the Soviet Union alone brought death to more than 24 million people, were put out of business by three naked, inebriated men in a bathhouse.**

CONCLUSION

In the former Soviet Empire, this was the end of the delusion of Karl Marx. The Communists had promised freedom, equality, and prosperity, but had delivered slave labor camps, death, and misery.

In the world as a whole, according to the *Black Book of Communism* published by Harvard University Press, the total number of victims of Communism is close to 100 million — an ocean of blood.

Who were the people who had caused this unimaginable slaughter? Can they return?

Unfortunately, they had never left and are very much among us — they are the political or religious fanatics, who believe that they know how to save mankind from itself, and that trying to build their utopian world justifies slaughter of innocent millions.

The demise of the Soviet Union gave rise to an infinite number of explanations and conspiracy theories. Would it have happened without Gorbachev? Without Yeltsin? Without both being there at the same time? Was the fall of the Communist regime due to the spiritual crisis caused by a discrepancy between the rosy propaganda and totalitarian reality, that made the Soviet people lose faith in the system? Or was it the United States policy of competition in armament?

According to one conspiracy theory, the CIA had bribed and manipulated the key players. But the theory that takes the prize, came from a former Deputy Minister of Culture in Brezhnev's administration, whom I met at a dinner party. In all seriousness, he handed me a manuscript in which he wrote that the real reason Gorbachev and Yeltsin destroyed the Soviet Union, was because their wives wanted to be able to shop in foreign countries.

The big unanswered question after the fall of Communism remains: why no one, not the learned professors of Sovietology, not the CIA or the intelligence services of other countries, not the think tanks or the diplomats, were able to foresee this pivotal historical event. Only President Regan prophesied that Bolshevism was heading onto the scrap heap of history, and it was he who convinced Gorbachev that the United States had no hostile intentions and it was safe for him to try to reform the system.

AFTERWORD

YELTSIN: A TRIAL DEMOCRACY

Unlike Gorbachev, who had intended to preserve the state control of major industries, Yeltsin wanted to transform the centrally planned economy into a free-market one. The question was whether to do it gradually or rapidly? He turned for advice to Western economists and institutions such as the International Monetary Fund, the World Bank, and the U.S. Treasury Department, which had developed procedures for such transformation in some former Soviet satellite countries. These procedures were known as "Shock Therapy," and were a combination of measures to decontrol prices and to stabilize the state's budget.

To counteract the inflation that exploded after the government price controls ended, Yeltsin raised taxes and increased interest rates to a high level; he also cut government subsidies to construction and to welfare, which created an economic depression that was worse than the one in the United States in the 1930s. The Gross Domestic Product fell by 50 percent, unemployment skyrocketed, hyperinflation wiped out personal savings and pensions, and tens of millions of people became destitute. Because many towns in the Soviet Union were built around a single employer, when that company collapsed, the major source of peoples' income disappeared and in February of 1992, Russia's Vice President called Yeltsin's program an "economic genocide."

In late 1992, Yeltsin launched a program of privatization of industry, and Russian citizens received vouchers with a nominal value of 10,000 rubles for purchase of shares in selected state enterprises. However, within months, most of the vouchers wound up in the hands of speculators, who together with the former Communist managers of companies, accumulated them by offering the starving people immediate cash, and became owners of the companies, known as the oligarchs.

In 1993, Yeltsin announced that to implement the needed reforms, he was going to assume special powers. He decided to disband the Congress and to rule by decree until the new elections and a referendum on a new constitution that would give him additional powers, could be passed. On the following day, the Congress declared Yeltsin removed from the presidency for violating the Constitution, and swore in the Vice President to be acting President. The delegates who supported this move then staged a sit-in in the White House. They were armed and determined to defend it against Yeltsin and his supporters.

There were mass demonstrations with tens of thousands of people protesting the terrible living conditions, the rise in violent crime, corruption, and collapsing medical services. The government employees and pensioners had not been paid for several months, and there was a scarcity of food and fuel. Yeltsin was blamed for everything, and in his memoir *The Struggle for Russia*, he admits suffering from depression, insomnia, and severe headaches.

By early October, Yeltsin had secured the support of the army and the Interior Ministry, and now, unlike in 1991, it was he who wanted to storm the White House and had it surrounded by tanks. When the protesting delegates refused to leave, the tanks opened fire killing more than a hundred and causing severe damage to the building. When troops entered the building, the defenders surrendered. Their leaders, including the former Vice President, were arrested, but in the interest of social peace, within a few months all were amnestied.

Yeltsin's government dissolved the Supreme Soviet, but in the elections to the newly named Federal Assembly, the Communists got about 25 percent of the votes and together with nationalists overwhelmed Yeltsin's supporters. The reason so many had voted for Communists was that after the death of Stalin there was a period of relative stability and, while the standard of living was low, the situation was better than the chaos, uncertainty, and deprivation they were experiencing now. The crime rate had skyrocketed and mafia gangs were extorting businesses and battled one another in the streets. In the mind of the people, their suffering was due to Yeltsin's democracy, which had weakened the strong hand of the government needed to keep law and order.

In 1994, the Autonomous Republic of Chechnya declared its independence from Russia, and since the Russian Federation (the new name of Russian Republic) consisted of eighty-nine autonomous regions, some close to Moscow, letting Chechnya secede would have created a precedent that could potentially have destroyed the whole Federation. To prevent this, in December 1994 Yeltsin ordered a military invasion of Chechnya, that led to approximately 15,000 civilian deaths and the destruction of the Chechnyan capital Grozny. In 1996, a peace agreement allowed Chechnya somewhat greater autonomy than it had before, but not full independence.

In 1995, Yeltsin's government desperately needed money to fund its operations and the growing foreign debt, and a banker named Potatin proposed a solution called "loans for shares." Private Banks such as Potatin's own Export-Import Bank, would make loans to the government and take shares of state-owned companies as security. If the government failed to repay the loan within a year, the shares would be sold at auction.

In 1996, for a $130 million loan to the government, Potatin's bank got the right to manage for one year fifty-one percent of the shares of a large oil company called Sidanco. Since the government could not repay the loan on time, the shares were sold at auction. But Potatin had arranged the conditions of the sale in such a way that the winner had to integrate the oil company with a refinery, and Potatin's bank just happened to own one.

In February 1996, Yeltsin, who had been recovering from his latest heart attack, and whose popularity was down to only about two percent, announced that he would run for a second term. His Communist opponents had a large disciplined organization and were appealing to memories of the old days of Soviet strength, international prestige, and domestic order. But Yeltsin, even though he was bed-ridden and needed a bypass operation, was not one to give up, and created a new centrist party which he called the Unity Party. He also got a team of media and financial oligarchs to bankroll the campaign, which guaranteed favorable media coverage and reminded the public of the threat of Communist return to power which could lead to civil war. In return for their support, the oligarchs were allowed to acquire majority stakes in valuable state-owned assets.

Yeltsin won by fifty-four percent against the Communists' forty. The other six percent voted "against all." Later that year, Yeltsin had the bypass operation that instead of being the anticipated quadruple, ended up quintuple, and he remained in the hospital for months. On the day of the operation, he signed a decree transferring his presidential power to the Vice President, but returning it to him not on the next day as was usual, but immediately upon his regaining consciousness. This was a clear sign that he did not have much faith in his Vice President.

To help the Russian Federation, the International Monetary Fund granted it $40 billion, most of which, according to Yeltsin's opponents, was stolen by Yeltsin's people and wound up in foreign banks. Many foreign advisers were helping with the privatization process, and some were also helping themselves by investing in enterprises which they knew would be receiving financing. According to insiders, Russian officials were requesting advisors' help primarily because a large part of the money allocated for them could be easily stolen.

In spite of all the help from abroad, in 1998 the Russian Federation ran out of money and defaulted on its debts, causing the financial market to panic and the Russian ruble to collapse. While the government was digging itself out of the hole by refinancing the debt, the crisis also had some positive effect by halting imports, which helped the development of domestic industries that had been unable to compete with the less expensive foreign goods.

Yeltsin enjoyed dealing with foreign affairs. It was quite an accomplishment for a former provincial Russian boy to be received by, and to receive, Queen Elizabeth of Great Britain and King Carlos of Spain, and be treated as an equal by presidents of powerful countries. He signed an arms limitation agreement with President George H. W. Bush, whom he found to be sympathetic and helpful.

But the Russian relations with the United States deteriorated when in 1999, hoping to prevent a slaughter as the Muslim Kosovo region tried to secede from the Russian ally Christian Serbia, the U.S. Air Force bombed the Serbs. Sometime later, when President Clinton demanded that the Russians cease bombing Chechnya that wanted to secede from Russia, Yeltsin thought him to be hypocritical, and there was no love lost between them.

In an interview in 1995, Clinton claimed that on a visit to Washington, Yeltsin was found on Pennsylvania Avenue in his underwear, drunk, trying to hail a cab to get pizza. But according to a former Russian prime minister, Yeltsin's behavior was caused by the strong drugs given to him by Kremlin doctors. Also, a Dutch neurosurgeon revealed that he had been secretly flown to Moscow to perform an operation for a neurological disorder that affected Yeltsin's sense of balance and made him wobble as if he were drunk.

On August 9, 1999, Yeltsin for the fourth time fired his entire cabinet, including the prime minister. He did not see anyone among the squabbling Moscow politicians who could take his place, and decided to bring in a younger, stronger, and more energetic outsider who could stand up to the politicians, the oligarchs, and the mafias. He found such a man in Vladimir Putin, who had a Doctorate in Economics and as a KGB spy in East Germany analyzed the political and economic situation in the country and recruited local agents. To test him, Yeltsin made him the head of the FSB, the Federal Security Service — one of the successor agencies of the KGB.

Putin passed the test, and to give him an advantage in the coming election, Yeltsin appointed him Prime Minister.

However, Putin did not have his own party organization, which put him at a disadvantage in competing against the Communist candidate. Therefore, Yeltsin organized a new centrist party, which he named United Russia. He had his researchers identify the most popular middle-of-the-road people in each electoral district, and convinced many of them to join the new party.

Then, to give Putin a head start, on December 31, 1999, Yeltsin unexpectedly resigned, and made Putin Acting President. According to Russian law, if the President should resign, the election to replace him must take place within three months, so that while Putin's opponents were preparing for the election scheduled for June, it took place in March.

In his New Year's Eve resignation address to the nation, Yeltsin apologized to the Russian people:

> Russia must enter the new millennium with new politicians, with new faces, with new, smart, strong, energetic people. And we, who have been in power for many years already, we must go. . . . I want to ask you for forgiveness. For the fact that many of the dreams we shared did not come true. And for the fact that what seemed simple to us, turned out to be tormentingly difficult. I ask forgiveness for not justifying some hopes for those people who believed that at one stroke, in one spurt, we could leap from the gray, stagnant, totalitarian past into the light, rich, civilized future. I myself believed in this that we could overcome everything in one spurt.
>
> Today it's important for me to tell you. The pain of each of you has called for pain in me, in my heart. Sleepless nights, tormenting worries

— about what needed to be done, so that people could live more easily and better. I did not have any more important task. I am leaving. I did all I could.

Yeltsin was a larger-than-life personality. In five years he rose from a provincial Communist apparatchik to the man who exploded the Communist Empire. In spite of his heart condition, he had unlimited energy and was not afraid to take chances. In his memoir, he tells that he had derived a great thrill from heading his car at high speed toward a tree and swerving at the very last moment. In one such case, his bodyguard jumped out of the car and almost got killed. Having been disappointed in his aides during his first term, Yeltsin became authoritarian during the second, making more and more decisions personally, and was referred to as Tsar Boris.

PUTIN: THE END OF DEMOCRACY

Vladimir Putin was born in Leningrad in 1952. His father was with the secret police and his mother was a factory worker. His grandfather had been a cook at Lenin's dacha. While in college, Putin joined the Communist Party and remained a member until it was dissolved.

Upon graduation he joined the KGB, and while using the cover of being a police officer, monitored foreign and consular officials. Later his duty was to combat political dissidents, and afterwards he was transferred to foreign intelligence. From 1985 to 1990 he was stationed in East Germany, where he kept an eye on German officials and recruited agents. After the Berlin Wall had fallen, Putin destroyed KGB documents and returned to Leningrad. He was assigned to the International Affairs Section of a University, where he maintained surveillance of students and recruited agents. He resigned from the KGB in August 1991, when it became involved in the coup against Gorbachev.

Putin was appointed the head of the Committee for External Relations of the St. Petersburg Mayor's Office, to promote international investments. He was investigated for issuing an export permit for a $93 million shipment of non-ferrous metals in exchange for food aid from abroad, but the food had never arrived. The investigators recommended that he be fired, but he remained on the job until 1996, when he went to Moscow and became Chief of the Presidential Property Management Department. Here he was noticed by Yeltsin, who appointed him deputy Chief of his Presidential Staff. In 1997, at the Mining Institute, he defended his Ph.D. dissertation in economics.

When Yeltsin told Putin he wanted to appoint him to the post of prime minister and to become his successor as President, Putin hesitated, saying that he did not think he was ready for the job, and Yeltsin gave him a day to make up his mind. When Putin accepted, the State Duma approved his appointment with 233 in favor, 84 against, and 17 abstentions. This made him the fifth Prime Minister in less than eighteen months, and few expected him to last longer than his predecessors. But Putin's law-and-order image and his firm stand on the war in Chechnya increased his popularity.

On Stalin's birthday in 1999, at an assembly of the heads of all parties newly elected to the parliament, Putin offered a toast to Stalin, in which he was joined by all but one attendee. Later he said that the disintegration of the Soviet Union was the greatest tragedy of the twentieth century.

Upon Yeltsin's resignation on December 31, 1999, Putin assumed the office of President, and, according to rumors, the first decree he signed was *"On guarantees for the former president of the Russian Federation and members of his family."* It assured that corruption charges against Yeltsin and his relatives would not be pursued.

One of the big problems that made Russia virtually ungovernable was the independence of the governors of various regions, some of whom became similar to warlords, complete with their own militias and even foreign relations departments. In Tatarstan, a predominantly Muslim autonomous region only about 400 miles from Moscow, Saudi Arabian mullahs were allowed to set up religious schools in which they preached the extreme form of Islam. The same thing happened in other Muslim areas, including Chechnya, where Al Qaeda had sent foreign fighters. The governors of these areas could not be replaced by elections because they controlled them, and removing them by force could have caused ethnic unrest. To gain control of the situation, Putin issued a decree dividing the country into seven federal administrative districts, each governed by a super-governor whom he appointed.

Little by little, much of the national media fell under Putin's control either by government takeover or through control by Putin-friendly oligarchs. While at the beginning of his first term there were puppet shows on television making fun of Putin, by the end of it they were all gone. Several reporters who were investigating corruption in the government and the conduct of the war in Chechnya were assassinated, but their cases were never solved.

While Putin did not interfere with the oligarchs who supported him, he was merciless with those who did not. The head of the oil company Yukos, Michail Khodorkovsky, who had supported Putin's opponents, wound up being prosecuted for fraud, embezzlement, and tax evasion.

He was sentenced to five years in prison, and then to another five years on additional charges. This was popular with many Russian people because the oligarchs were considered to have stolen the companies and now were profiting from selling out national resources. However, Putin's opponents and the international press saw it as punishment for Khodorkovsky's political activity.

Putin's renationalization of large companies and the natural resources led to the description of the Russian system as state capitalism, but Putin's administration describes it as a "Sovereign Democracy" that takes into account the needs of the country. In the economy, the share of oil and gas in Russia's Gross Domestic Product rose above thirty percent and constituted sixty-five percent of its exports, which made Russian economy very sensitive to fluctuation of the price of oil.

During Putin's first term in office, the price of oil rose, and eventually accounted for nearly fifty percent of the budget. As a result, pensions were paid, the unemployment decreased, and the standard of living improved. Therefore, in March 2004 Putin was re-elected by seventy-one percent of the vote, and his United Russia Party dominated the political life of the country. As oil prices continued to rise during his second term, Russia paid off its foreign debt, and Moscow became a busy European City with fashionable boutiques and growing middle class. But not everything was going smoothly. According to Andrew Jack's book *Inside Putin's Russia:* "The proportion of firms frequently forced to give bribes rose from 30.6 percent in 1999, to 38.7 percent in 2002. ... The Kremlin's own Control Department concluded in 2003 that bribes were widespread and regulations threatened the survival of small businesses."

To justify his rule, Putin began changing the official attitude toward the past, and a manual for history teachers titled *A Modern History of Russia,* which Putin said would "help instill young people with a sense of pride in Russia," was published in June 2007. It portrayed Stalin as a strict but successful leader.

In international affairs, Putin's objective was to re-establish Russia as a great power and to prevent Ukraine from joining NATO. While he had been increasingly critical of the United States and other Western countries, after the September 11, 2001 attack Putin allowed establishment of American military bases in Central Asia that were needed for supplying US forces in Afghanistan. In April 2008, Putin was included in the *Time* magazine's list of 100 most influential people in the world.

Unlike Gorbachev, who tried to limit production of vodka, Putin put his name on a vodka brand — Putinka. There is also Putin brand of canned foods, Putin caviar, and Putin T-shirts. According to Putin's opponents, he also owns a substantial percentage of several oil companies, which would make him the richest man in Russia.

Since the Russian constitution limits the president to two consecutive terms, in 2008, Putin endorsed his long-time collaborator, Prime Minister Dmitry Medvedev, as a candidate for the presidency and Medvedev won the election with seventy-one percent of the popular vote. He in turn appointed Putin as the Prime Minister of Russia, and Putin continued to run the country. At the end of Medvedev's term, he did not run against Putin for a second term, and in 2012 Putin again was elected President and again made Medvedev his Vice President. There is no reason to think that this game will not be played over and over again, making Putin effectively President for life, and completing the circle of Russian history from a Tsar for life to a President for life.

LIST OF MAJOR NAMES

1. Marx, Karl – The principal creator of the idea of Communism.

2. Lenin, Vladimir – The first Communist Dictator and a mass murderer.

3. Stalin, Joseph – The second Communist Dictator and a mass murderer.

4. Trotsky, Leon – Organizer of the Red Army and a mass murderer.

5. Dzerzhinski, Feliks – Organizer of the secret police and a mass murderer.

6. Beria, Lavrenti – Head of the KGB and a mass murderer; executed by Khrushchev.

7. Khrushchev, Nikita – A mass murderer; loved Lenin, hated Stalin.

8. Gorbachev, Mikhail – The reformer and last president of the Soviet Union.

9. Bukharin, Nikolai – A favorite of Lenin; executed by Stalin.

10. Engels, Friedrich – He and Karl Marx created the idea of Communism.

11. Kaganovich, Lazar – Stalin's toady and a mass murderer.

12. Kamenev, Lev – Lenin's favorite associate; executed by Stalin.

13. Kirov, Sergei – Possible Stalin's rival; probably killed by Stalin.

14. Malenkov, Georgi – Stalin's toady and a mass murderer.

15. Molotov, Vyacheslav – Stalin's toady and a mass murderer.

16. Putin, Vladimir – The second President of Russia. A semi-dictator.

17. Radek, Karl – Lenin's associate; executed by Stalin.

18. Rykov, Alexei – Lenin's associate; executed by Stalin.

19. Yagoda, Genrikh – Head of the secret police; executed by Yezhov and a mass murderer.

20. Yeltsin, Boris – The first President of Russia. Democratic reformer.

21. Yezhov, Nikolai – Head of the secret police; executed by Beria.

22. Zinoviev, Grigory – Lenin's associate; executed by Stalin and a mass murderer.

GLOSSARY

Apparatchik – A member of the governing clique.

Bolsheviks – Communists dedicated to establishing dictatorship of the proletariat.

Bourgeoisie – Middle-class people whom the Bolsheviks wanted to exterminate.

Communism – An ideology advocating the elimination of private property by force, as opposed to **Socialism** that advocated the elimination of private property by democratic means. To disguise their violent intentions, the Communists and the Nazis misleadingly and confusingly called themselves Socialists.

Cominform – Worldwide Communist propaganda organization.

Comintern – Communist International – a worldwide Communist organization.

Commissar – Communist of ministerial rank. Also, a political-military officer.

Coup – Violent overthrow of an existing government by a small group.

Dacha – A country home.

Duma – The Russian Parliament before the Revolution.

Gestapo – Hitler's secret police.

KGB (Cheka, GPU, OGPU, NKVD) – Different names of the Soviet secret police.

Kolkhoz – A Soviet collective farm.

Komsomol – A Soviet Youth organization.

Kulaks – Well-to-do farmers.

Nazi – Member of the German National-Socialist Party.

Oligarch – In Russia, someone who illegally gained control of a company.

Panzer – A German tank.

Politburo –The seven top Communists who controlled the Soviet Union.

Presidium of the Communist Party – Another name for the Politburo.

Proletariat – Working class that owns very little.

Rule by fiat – Governing by command.

Sabotage – Deliberate damaging of equipment or undermining an activity.

Socialism – (See "Communism")

SS (Schutzstaffel) – German elite army units.

Troika – Soviet court consisting of three Communist judges.

Tsar (also spelled Czar) –The Emperor of Russia.

U.S.S.R. – Union of Soviet Socialist Republics.

Utopia – An impossible ideal society.

Bibliography

In addition to Google and Wikipedia, the following sources were consulted or quoted:

1. Stephane Courtois, *The Black Book of Communism*, Harvard University Press, 1999

2. David Remnick, *Lenin's Tomb: The Last Days of the Soviet Empire*, Vantage, 1994

3. Anne Appelbaum, *Gulag: A History*, Anchor Books, 2004

4. Donald Rayfield, *Stalin and His Hangmen*, Random House, 2004

5. William Taubman, *Khrushchev: The Man and His Era*, Norton, 2003

6. Edward Crankshaw, *Khrushchev Remembers*, Little, Brown & Co., 1970

7. William Z. Foster, "The American Soviet Government," in *Communism in America: A History in Documents*, edited by Alfred Fried, Columbia University Press, 1997

8. Alan Bullock, *Hitler and Stalin*, Vantage Books, 1993

9. Svetlana Alliluyeva, *Only One Year*, Harper, 1970

10. J.V. Stalin, *Problems of Leninism*, Foreign Languages Press, Peking, 1976

11. General von Manstein, *Lost Victories*, Presidio Press, 1982

12. Mikhail Gorbachev, *Perestroika*, Harper, 1987

13. Hendrick Smith, *The New Russians*, Avon Books, 1991

14. Sidney Hook, *World Communism*, Van Nostrand, 1962

15. Anna Larina, *This I Cannot Forget*, Norton, 1993

16. Leon Trotsky, *My Life*, Scribner, 1930

17. Mark Lilla, *The Reckless Mind*, N.Y. Review of Books, 2001

18. Victor Kravchenko, *I Chose Freedom*, Scribner, 1946

19. Joseph Davies, *Mission to Moscow*, Reader's League, 1941

20. George Orwell, *Homage to Catalonia*, Harcourt, 1952

21. Vassily Grossman, *Life and Fate*, Harvill, 1986

22. Howard Fast, *The Naked God*, Praeger, 1957

23. Robert Reeves, *President Kennedy: Profile of Power*, Touchstone, 1993

24. Andrei Gromyko, *Memoirs*, Hutchinson, 1989

25. Alexander Solzhenitsyn, *One Day in the Life of Ivan Denisovich*, Dutton, 1963

26. Nadezhda Mandelstam, *Hope Against Hope*, Modern Library, 1970

27. Lev Kopelev, *The Education of a True Believer*, Harper, 1980

28. Evgenia Ginsburg, *Journey Into the Whirlwind*, Harcourt, 1967

29. Walter Laqueur, *Stalin: The Glasnost Revelations*, Scribner, 1990

30. Amy Knight, *Who Killed Kirov?* Hill and Wang, 1999

31. Dusko Doder, *Gorbachev: Heretic in the Kremlin*, Viking Penguin, 1990

32. Leon Aron, *Yeltsin: A Revolutionary Life*, St. Martin's Press, 2000

33. Jan Valtin, *Out of the Night*, Alliance Book Corp., 1941

34. Norman Davies, *No Simple Victory*, Penguin Books, 2006

35. Andrew Jack, *Inside Putin's Russia,* Oxford University Press, 2004

36. Anatole Konstantin, *Through the Eyes of an Immigrant,* K. Memoirs, 2016

37. Anatole Konstantin, *A Red Boyhood: Growing Up Under Stalin,* Missouri University Press, 2008

38. Wikimedia Commons, Portraits of Historical Figures

39. Dutch National Archives, Portrait of Nikita Khrushchev

ACKNOWLEDGMENTS

In writing *A Brief History of Communism: The Rise and Fall of the Soviet Empire,* I am greatly indebted to the authors of the books listed in the "Bibliography," especially to those of *The Black Book of Communism* and of *Lenin's Tomb: The Last Days of the Soviet Empire.*

I also thank my grandson Miles, who designed the covers and was helpful with technical aspects of putting together the book, as well as my son David, and Francesca Begos who helped with editing.

ABOUT THE AUTHOR

Anatole Konstantin grew up in Ukraine when it was part of the Soviet Union ruled by Stalin. In 1938, when Anatole was ten years old, his father was arrested by the KGB and the family never heard about him until fifty years later when Gorbachev came to power and they received a letter from the KGB saying that he had been executed and was now being posthumously rehabilitated. This was an admission that he had been innocent.

Upon his father's arrest, the family became "enemies of the people" and barely survived. In 1941 when Germany attacked the Soviet Union, Anatole with his mother and little brother escaped several days before the Germans occupied their town and they became refugees in the Soviet Republic of Kazakhstan in Central Asia. In spite of misery and near starvation, Anatole managed to go to school, and when WW II ended, the family escaped to Poland and then to West Germany where he became a student at the Technical University of Munich.

When he graduated as a Mechanical Engineer, the United States was admitting 200,000 Displaced Persons and he came to the land of his dreams. After having worked for twenty years in several companies, Anatole started an engineering consulting company which later became the PDC International Corp. that manufactures packaging machinery. His book, *A RED BOYHOOD – Growing Up Under Stalin*, describes life under Communist dictatorship and his escape from it. He also taught a course on The Rise and Fall of the Soviet Empire at the Lifetime Learners Institute at the Norwalk Community College.

PRAISE FOR *A Red Boyhood: Growing Up Under Stalin*

"What makes Konstantin's recollections so captivating is his ability to effectively divide the text between small details vividly rendered, such as a trip to the movie theater, and the larger story of a global political and military struggle."

Kirkus Reviews

"Replete with the perils of living under Communism and in wartime, Konstantin's lucid memoir contributes to the body of civilian witness to World War II."

Gilbert Taylor

"This is praise for your writing, because once I started, I couldn't put it down, and gave it to Laura, who had the same experience. You evoke a world that will be forever remembered because, despite the pain and horrors of it, you recreate it beautifully, sensually, and with affection.

Even now, weeks after reading your book, we recall a bit or other of wisdom from it, with the story it came in, and it makes us happy all over again. You wrote a masterwork. I already lent the book to a friend."

Andrei Godrescu

Novelist, screenwriter, commentator for NPR

"I finished the book you sent us a few days ago and wanted to thank you again for having given me the occasion to learn about your friend's fate and that of so many others at the time through his captivating narration. His description of what he finds in the small towns in the Ukraine where he lived before the war are overwhelming and I often think about his stories."

"On the strength of [a] recommendation I bought the book and read every word of it. What a fascinating description of his boyhood! The author has an excellent talent for description! I could closely empathize with his life and encounters and the many insecurities and threats he confronted. . . . I really enjoyed the book and want to thank you for the 'heads up.'"

PRAISE FOR *Through the Eyes of an Immigrant*

"It establishes Konstantin as an extraordinary moral witness who faithfully recorded depredations that man visited upon his fellow man in the name of ideology."

AWARDS FOR *Through the Eyes of an Immigrant:*

1. The Connecticut Press Club 2017 award: FIRST PLACE in nonfiction books.

2. NFPW 2017 Communication Contest: SECOND PLACE in biography or autobiography.

"I wish I had known about this book when I was teaching American History 102. . . . The combination of one man's story and a careful documentation to back up the author's points, makes this book both compelling and useful."

Comment by the contest judge